SOLDIERS OF 1814

*American Enlisted Men's Memoirs
Of The Niagara Campaign*

by
Jarvis Hanks
Amasiah Ford
and
Alexander McMullen

· · · · · · · ·

Edited,
with an
Introduction and Notes
by
Donald E. Graves

· · · · · · · · ·

Illustrated
by
George Balbar

· · · · · · · · ·

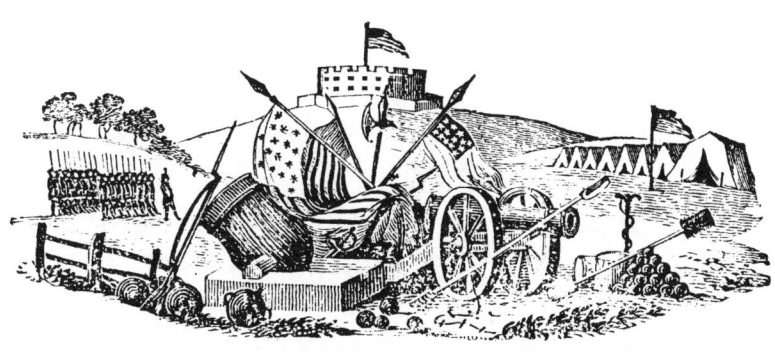

©1995
**OLD FORT NIAGARA ASSOCIATION, INC,
YOUNGSTOWN, NEW YORK**
ISBN: 0-941967-16-6

This publication is made possible by a grant from:
New York State Society
The National Society, United States Daughters of 1812

For

Erica Dolores Greaves,
the Angelito,

and

Wilfrid William John Greaves,
the Not-So-Little Drummer Boy

Table of Contents

page

Acknowledgements 4

Introduction: The Enlisted Men of the Left Division, 1814 5

Editor's Note 16

Part I - The Memoir of Drummer Jarvis Frary Hanks, 11th Infantry 19
   1. Early Life and Decision to Enlist 19
   2. First Months in the Army 23
   3. The Campaign on the St. Lawrence, 1813-1814 26
   4. Scott's Camp at Buffalo, April-May 1814 28
   5. The Campaign on the Niagara: Chippawa and Lundy's Lane 32
   6. The Siege of Fort Erie, August to September 1814 38
   7. The End of the War 45

Part II - The Memoir of Private Amasiah Ford, 23rd Infantry 51
   1. Campaign of 1813 51
   2. Lundy's Lane and the Niagara, July 1814 53
   3. The Siege of Fort Erie, August to September 1814 55
   4. The End of the War 58

Part III - The Narrative of Private Alexander McMullen, Fenton's
Regiment of Pennsylvania Volunteers 61
   1. Call to Service and the March to Erie 61
   2. The Raid on Long Point, Canada 63
   3. An Act of Mutiny and the Camp at Buffalo 66
   4. The Battle of Chippawa 68
   5. The Battle of Lundy's Lane 71
   6. The Retreat to Fort Erie 75

About the Editor 80

Acknowledgements

The editor and the Old Fort Niagara Association would like to express their gratitude to the Buffalo and Erie County Historical Society for permission to reproduce the memoir of Jarvis Hanks; to the Lundy's Lane Historical Society for permission to reproduce the memoir of Alexander McMullen; and to Cowles Magazines and the United States Military History Institute of Carlisle, Pennsylvania, for permission to reproduce the memoir of Amasiah Ford.

Introduction

The Enlisted Men of the Left Division, 1814

In the early morning hours of July 3, 1814, drummer boy Jarvis Hanks of the 11th United States Infantry, a sleepy fourteen-year-old native of Pawlet, Vermont, splashed ashore from a crowded boat on the Niagara River and invaded Canada. Accompanying him that night, and in the days that followed, was the remainder of the Left Division of the United States Army: four generals, a dozen or so colonels, two brigades of regular infantry, one brigade of militia, a battalion of artillery and their field pieces, a company of light dragoons, nearly five hundred Indian warriors, more than four hundred horses, and many, many wagons. During the next 113 days, Jarvis (along with his division) would participate in the hardest-fought military operation of the War of 1812 — the Niagara campaign of 1814 — and, to the end of his life, he would remember the scenes of carnage he witnessed as a young adolescent during a long and bloody summer.

Jarvis Hanks would be just another name on a document, a faceless cypher like so many of his fellow soldiers, except that he left a memoir of his wartime experiences for the benefit of his descendants. Fortunately, he was not the only enlisted man of Major General Jacob Brown's Left Division who possessed the instinct to record — Private Amasiah Ford of the 23rd Infantry and Private Alexander McMullen of Fenton's Regiment of Pennsylvania Volunteers also compiled accounts of their military life. Assembled here together for the first time, these historical memoirs provide a colorful picture of a memorable campaign from the point of view of three young men, one from each of the three brigades of the division. They are valuable items, as accounts of the Niagara campaign by the enlisted men of either side are very rare.[1]

---

[1] This author knows of only three eyewitness accounts of the 1814 Niagara campaign by British *enlisted* personnel: the "Journal of the Rev. George Ferguson" (private in the 100th Regiment of Foot) held by the United Church Archives in Toronto, Ontario; Norman C. Lord (ed.), "The War of 1812 on the Canadian Frontier, 1812-1814. Letters Written by Sgt. James Comins, 8th Foot", *Journal of the Society for Army Historical Research,* XVIII (1939), pp. 199-211; and the "Recollections" of Private Shadrach Byfield of the 41st Regiment of Foot in John Gelner (ed.), *Recollections of the War of 1812: Three Eyewitness Accounts* (Toronto, 1964).

Eyewitness accounts by officers and non-regular personnel are much more plentiful. See the relevant sections of John C. Fredriksen (ed.), *Free Trade and Sailor's Rights. A Bibliography of the War of 1812* (Westport, CT, 1985) and *Shield of Republic/Sword of Empire. A Bibliography of United States Military Affairs, 1783-1846* (Westport, 1990).

The original of Jarvis Hanks's manuscript was acquired by the Buffalo and Erie County Historical Society in the late 1950s. Portions of it, edited by Lester W. Smith, appeared in the periodical, *Niagara Frontier,* in 1960.[2] Amasiah Ford's memoir is part of the *American History Illustrated* collection of the United States Army Military History Institute at Carlisle, Pennsylvania and has never before appeared in print. McMullen's account was published in the late 1890s as part of the second volume of Ernest Cruikshank's *Documentary History of the Campaign Upon the Niagara Frontier.* The present whereabouts of the original manuscript is unknown and even the published version has become a scarce item.[3]

Each of the three memoirs differs according the experiences and personality of its author. Jarvis Hanks was just thirteen years old when an army recruiting party marched through his little village in the spring of 1813 and he convinced his parents to give their consent to his enlistment as a drummer — a consent given on the understanding that the lad would only be employed on the recruiting service, not in battle.

Such promises are as easily broken as they are given and, five months later, Jarvis saw his first action at Crysler's Farm in 1813, before fighting the following year at Chippawa, Lundy's Lane and Fort Erie. By the end of his military service in May 1815, Hanks felt at home in the army and considered going to the military academy at West Point but was dissuaded by his father. Following the war, he pursued a somewhat gypsy existence as a freelance house, furniture and portrait painter, medical student and teacher before marrying and raising a family. He died at Cleveland, Ohio, in 1858.[4]

From notes in the manuscript, Hanks apparently worked on his memoir from 1831 to 1847. It is a colorful and well-written document, full of anecdotes and unconscious irony. Jarvis made the best of his time in the army but, in hindsight, was somewhat resentful of the ease with which his father agreed to let him enlist. Although he never clearly states it as such, it appears that the young drummer boy was something of a "mascot" in the 11th Infantry and was

---

[2] Lester W. Smith (ed.), "A Drummerboy in the War of 1812: The Memoirs of Jarvis Frary Hanks", *Niagara Frontier,* VII (1960), pp. 53-62.

[3] Ernest A. Cruikshank, *Documentary History of the Campaign Upon the Niagara Frontier in 1814,* (Welland, Ont., n.d. [c.1896-1898]), II, pp. 368-379. At the time of publication, the original of McMullen's narrative was stated by Cruikshank to be in the possession of "W.H.S. McMullen of Crete, Pennsylvania". Inquiries by the editor to the Pennsylvania Historical Society and various historical societies in Franklin County have failed to turn up this manuscript.

[4] The original manuscript of Hanks' memoir contains a considerable amount of material on his postwar life that, for reasons of length, has been omitted here. The original may be consulted at the Buffalo and Erie County Historical Society, Buffalo, New York.

watched over by both his officers and the older, and steadier, enlisted men. Religious in his later years, Jarvis attributed his "hairbreadth escapes in battles, almost fatal accidents, [and] preservation from open vice and capital sins" to divine intervention. In Jarvis's opinion, his survival was a "near run thing". The reader will probably agree with him.

Amasiah Ford was a private in the 23rd Infantry of Brigadier General Eleazar W. Ripley's Second Brigade. A native of Saratoga County, New York, he enlisted in February 1813 at the age of seventeen. His memoir, written some thirty-four years after the war, is not as polished as the work of either Hanks or McMullen, but its account of seemingly endless marches, inclement weather, short rations and occasional combat is compelling in its starkness. Unlike Hanks and McMullen, Ford, a very straightforward individual, never doubts for a moment the rightness of his cause, the intelligence of his generals, or the bravery of his officers and comrades. His is the simple story of a soldier who did his duty as ordered and was proud to do so.

Finally, from Brigadier General Peter B. Porter's Third Brigade, comes the account of Private Alexander McMullen of Fenton's Pennsylvania Volunteers. In contrast to Ford and Hanks, both regulars, McMullen never quite made a convincing adjustment to military life. His memoir is basically that of a civilian and, as a result, is delightfully honest and free of heroic posturing. This is particularly true of his description of the sanguinary battle of Lundy's Lane where many of his comrades "were contending for places in the rear" and McMullen feels his situation "to be an awful one."

Although McMullen and the other volunteer soldiers of the Third Brigade fight better than might be expected (considering they had only a few weeks of professional training at Buffalo under Winfield Scott), they refuse to carry out an order to remove the captured British artillery, "being tired out and half dead for want of water," and resent it when an officer criticizes their behavior as they felt "we had done all that men could do, and this was our thanks." McMullen laments the needless destruction of property he witnesses, particularly the shooting of a "fine English cow" that he and his farmer comrades admire. He is a rather gentle soul who is more than a little out of place in the army and we leave him still recovering from a bout with intermittent fever at the home of a congenial widow outside Buffalo in August 1814. Nothing is known about his postwar life.

Taken as a whole, the memoirs of Hanks, Ford, and McMullen go a long way to putting a human face on the private soldiers of the United States Army during the War of 1812. For we know little about these men beyond what can be gleaned from the extant military records. A recent study of the enlisted personnel of the army has concluded that more than 62,000 men served in its ranks during the years 1812-1815. The vast majority (86.8%) of those whose birthplace is known (including Ford, Hanks and McMullen) were native-born Americans while, of those who were foreign-born (13.1%), just over half came from Ireland. The mean age of recruits at enlistment was 26.8 years and of those who listed their peacetime occupations, most described themselves as "farmers" (39%) or "laborers" (14.2%). As the author of the study points out, however, many of these "farmers" were, in truth, "agricultural laborers", who owned no land.[5]

These conclusions have been confirmed by an intensive analysis of the records of the men of two infantry companies that served on the northern frontier in 1813-1814: Captain Lemuel Bradford's company of the 21st Infantry from Massachusetts and what is now Maine and Captain Daniel McFarland's company of the 22nd Infantry from Pennsylvania. In Bradford's company, of the 147 men for whom there is information, 106 (or 72%) described themselves as "farmers" or "laborers" while of McFarland's, 99 men, 43 (or 42%) listed similar occupations. The average age at enlistment in Bradford's company was 24.56 years while in McFarland's, it was 25.4 years.[6]

It would probably be safe to say that except for those (possibly very few) who enlisted out of patriotism (including Hanks and Ford but not McMullen), the vast majority of these men were forced into military service by the winds of economic change sweeping across the United States. One commentator has concluded that wartime recruits appear to have been men of "respectable social status" but "close to the margins of that respectability", who had felt the impact of economic dislocations brought about by the Embargo Acts, the pressure of population growth on the eastern seaboard and the restructuring of traditional artisan craft activities into early industrial manufactories.[7]

Other than two meals a day, however, the army provided little compensatory benefit. The monthly pay of an infantry private in 1814 was eight dollars; corporals received ten and sergeants and drummers (like Hanks) eleven dollars a month — this, in a time, when agricultural laborers were commonly paid between fifty cents and one dollar *per day*. Recognizing that enlisted pay was little inducement to recruiting, Congress increased bonuses and incentives throughout the war — by 1814, a recruit could expect to receive $124 bounty after mustering and 160 acres of land on leaving the service. Even these (for the time) generous terms had little appeal — as one Ohioan rather bluntly put it,

---

[5] John Stagg, "Enlisted Men in the United States Army, 1812-1815: A Preliminary Survey", *William and Mary Quarterly*, 3rd Series, XLIII (1986), pp. 615-45.

[6] Joseph Whitehorne, *While Washington Burned: The Battle of Fort Erie, 1814* (Baltimore, 1992), Annex O, "Profile of Typical U.S. Units."

[7] Stagg, "Enlisted Men", p. 645.

army pay was not enough for a man to "turn out to get himself killed." This same critic added a surprisingly modern sentiment about the pay of politicians when he "wished every member of Congress had 160 acres of land stuffed up his XXXX instead of receiving $6.00 per day." [8]

If pay was little incentive and patriotism was not widespread (for it was not a popular war), how did the army attract men? One way was by a display of military pomp and circumstance. The War Department advised officers on the recruiting service to include in their parties a drummer or other musicians and "a few handsome, well-dressed men, who, from their appearance and activity, may be enabled to give a spirit to the ... business." [9] It was the entry of just such a party into the hamlet of Pawlet in the spring of 1813 that caused young Jarvis Hanks to become "fired with ardour in anticipation of a soldier's career."

A surer, and more traditional, method was to buy all and sundry males a free drink or two at the local tavern, spin them a yarn of military glory and, before they got too sober, have them passed by a surgeon and put their signature or mark on the proper papers. Such a procedure caused many complaints (often from abandoned wives) and there was always a danger that the recruiting party would get too much into the spirit of the thing and annoy the local citizenry. One "Old Soldier" complained to the secretary of war about "a dissipated capt. H. walking from Tavern to Tavern and from shop to shop, drinking, singing, etc., soldiers about him following his example — capt. grosly [sic] rude and insulting in his deportment — soldiers equally so." [10]

Despite such sociable practises, recruits were hard to find and throughout the war the army's numbers were always far short of its authorized totals. Very early on, even the minimal standards of the peacetime army (5 feet, 6 inches of height and less than 35 years of age) went by the board. [11] By 1814, the only directions concerning recruits were that no man was to be enlisted who had

---

[8] Campbell to Worthington, June 17, 1812, Worthington Papers, Ohio State Library, quoted in John Stagg, *Mr. Madison's War* (Princeton, 1983), p. 163. On the pay of soldiers in 1814, see *The Army Register of the United States* (Boston, 1814), p. 106. On civilian wages during this period, see Joseph Walker (ed.), Pleasure and Business in Western Pennsylvania: The Journal of Joshua Gilpin, 1809 (Harrisburg, PA, 1975), pp. 84-85, cited in Stagg, *Mr. Madison's War,* p. 173.

[9] Recruiting Instructions, January 15, 1813, *An Act, Establishing Rules and Articles for the Government of the Armies of the United States with the Regulations of the War Department Respecting the Same* (Hereafter cited as *1812 Regulations;* Albany, 1812), pp. 32, 94.

[10] "Old Soldier" to Secretary of War, November 1812, National Archives, Record Group 107, micro 221, reel 47.

[11] "An Act fixing the Military Peace Establishment fo the United States", March 16, 1802, section 11, *1812 Regulations.*

"ulcerated legs, scalded head, rupture, or scurvy, or who is an habitual drunkard, or known to have epileptic fits." [12]

All potential recruits had to pass a medical examination, but it must have been of the most perfunctory sort as the War Department felt constrained to direct that surgeons were not to pass any man as fit "who has not stripped off all his clothes, to the end that it be ascertained as far as possible, that he has the perfect use of every joint and limb — that he has no tumors nor diseased enlargements of bones or joints, nor sore legs nor rupture." [13] Basically, the army took what it could get, and the result was that, too often, new recruits were "habitually intemperate, with constitutions broken down by inebriation and its consequent diseases; whose bloated countenance exhibited false and insidious marks of health." [14] The recruiting parties themselves may have had a similar appearance.

As soon as a recruiting officer had collected enough men, usually one hundred or so, he sent them either to a regimental rendezvous or to the regiment itself, and then went out to get more. This was the cause of much dissatisfaction among recruits as many regarded their enlistment as a personal contract between themselves and the officer who had enlisted them — they disliked serving under another man. They may have had a point, as it appears that companies recruited, trained and led on campaign by the same officer, such as Captain Azariah Odell's company of the 23rd Infantry (to which Ford belonged), possessed better unit cohesion and performed better in combat.

By one method or another, the army did get men. They enlisted for various terms of service — the most popular being "during the war" (the duration) although many signed on for the standard five-year term while others took advantage of the eighteen-month term offered in 1812 or the twelve-month term offered in early 1813. Drummer Hanks's regiment consisted of mostly wartime and five-year men and, naturally, there was much rejoicing among the former and much wailing among the latter when the news of peace was received in the spring of 1815.

After joining their regiments, new recruits were quickly inculcated into the mysteries of military life. If they had not already received them, they were now issued with uniforms, complete with a leather stock or neck band that held the soldier's head rigidly upright. They also received the tools of their trade — usually a variant of the .69 calibre Springfield musket and its attendant 15-inch bayonet — and set about learning how to use them. At Winfield Scott's camp

---

[12] Recruiting Regulations, May 2, 1814, *The Army Register of the United States* (Boston, 1814), p. 15.

[13] *Ibid.*

[14] James Mann, *Medical Sketches of the Campaigns of 1812, 13, 14* (Dedham, MA, 1816), p. 122.

of instruction in the spring of 1814, such training was incessant, beginning at first light and continuing until dark.[15]

The enlisted man's day at this camp was closely regulated by various drum signals. At "the first appearance of day", the assembled drummers of the camp beat "reveille". This was followed by a period of drill and then came "peas on a trencher", the breakfast call, at 7 A.M., followed by the "troop" for the calling of the roll and the issue of orders. At 12 noon, the men were summoned to their dinner by the beating of "roast beef". And so it went throughout the day until the evening roll call, the "retreat", shortly followed by "tattoo", the signal for the men to repair to their tents and remain there until morning.[16]

A stickler for detail, Scott paid particular attention to the appearance, cleanliness and deportment of his men. Their hair was to be "closely cut behind, so that no part of it shall be seen projecting over the Coat Collar" while, in front, "no part of it shall be seen hanging below the cap or Hat." [17] He allowed whiskers "but no part of them is to extend below a straight line, drawn from the lower corner of the ear, to the corner of the mouth on the same side of the face." His men were ordered to bathe regularly in Lake Erie in parties commanded by an officer who was to make sure that they were to "wash themselves from head to foot, but not to remain immersed in the water more than five minutes." [18]

Scott's interest extended down to what his men carried in their knapsacks. Soldiers of his First Brigade were to have, besides their uniforms, weapons and load-carrying equipment, only the following items: "one shirt, one pair Summer pantaloons, one pair shoes, one pair socks (or stockings), one fatigue frock, one pair trowzers and one blanket, a brush and pocket handkerchief may be added but nothing else."[19]

The rigorous daily schedule at Buffalo left soldiers little time for personal amusements. Toward the latter part of June 1814, some entertainment was

---

[15] For a description of the uniforms of the American soldier of the War of 1812, see René Chartrand, *Uniforms and Equipment of the United States Forces in the War of 1812* (Youngstown, NY, 1992), especially pp. 42-49. For a discussion of the training of the Left Division at Buffalo in the spring of 1814, see Donald E. Graves, *The Battle of Lundy's Lane: On the Niagara in 1814* (Baltimore, 1993), chapter 2.

[16] Alexander Smyth, *Regulations for the Field Exercise, Manoeuvres, and Conduct of the Infantry of the United States* (Philadelphia, 1812), pp. 175-76, 205; Brigade Order, June 17, 1814, Left Division Order Book, New York State Library, Albany, New York, MSS 11225.

[17] General Order, June 2, 1814, Left Division Order Book.

[18] Brigade Order, June 13, 1814, Left Division Order Book.

[19] Brigade Order, June 23, 1814, Left Division Order Book.

provided by the large contingent of native warriors attached to the division who entered the camp "trading moccasins, trinkets, &c. and some times running races, shooting with the bow and arrow, throwing the tomahawk, and shewing the war dance, at all of which diversions they are very expert."[20]

Although strictly forbidden, gambling was possibly the most popular form of amusement. Given the moral code of the times, however, it was not regarded as proper to go into action with the "Devil's devices" on one's person and men usually discarded them before battle. In the spring of 1814 an officer marching to an engagement recorded that he "saw more cards scattered along the roads this day than I has seen or will ever see again in my life put all together" as for "upwards of two miles the road was strewed with cards and in greater numbers to all appearance than the leaves of the trees."[21]

In the army of the War of 1812, as in perhaps all armies, mealtimes were the high points of the soldiers' day. Although the rations at Buffalo seem to have been of good quality, there were often complaints about the food. Jarvis Hanks was horrified to discover that he had exchanged the pleasures of his mother's table for army cuisine while Alexander McMullen complained that "the flour was mouldy and the beef and pork unfit to be eaten."

By regulation, each soldier was to receive daily one and a quarter pounds (including bones) of beef or three quarters of a pound of pork, eighteen ounces of bread or flour and a due proportion of salt, soap, vinegar and candles. If they had the money, they could eke out this bland diet with items purchased from the sutler, a vendor authorized to sell to the troops. In their search for profit, these merchants took many risks — in August and September 1814, some braved British artillery fire and entered the lines at Fort Erie to hawk their wares. Naturally, their prices were exorbitant. At Fort Meigs in the spring of 1813, the *authorized* sutlers' prices were 25 cents for bacon, 50 cents for soap or chocolate, 62 1/2 cents for coffee, and three dollars for molasses. At eight dollars a month (when they received their pay which was often months in arrears) few privates could afford these delicacies.[22]

In addition to food, each soldier also received, by regulation, a daily ration

---

[20] John C. Fredriksen (ed.), "The Pennsylvania Volunteers in the War of 1812: An Anonymous Journal of Service for the Year 1814", *Western Pennsylvania Historical Magazine*, LXX (1987), p. 149.

[21] John C. Fredriksen (ed.), "Chronicle of Valour: The Journal of a Pennsylvania Officer in the War of 1812", *Western Pennsylvania Historical Magazine*, LXVII (1984), pp. 245-46.

[22] Authorized rations from *1812 Regulations*, p. 52. Information on sutlers at Fort Erie from Joseph Whitehorne, "Fort Erie and U.S. Operations on the Niagara Frontier in 1814", in Susan Pfeiffer and Ronald Williamson (eds.), *Snake Hill: An Investigation of a Military Cemetery from the War of 1812* (Toronto, 1991), p. 39. Sutlers' prices at Fort Meigs from General Order, Camp Meigs, April 21, 1813, in Harlow Lindley (ed.), *Fort Meigs and the War of 1812* (Columbus, OH, 1975), p. 11.

of one gill (four ounces) of whiskey, rum or brandy. If authorized, the sutler would sell him additional liquor at the usual high prices — at Fort Meigs, whiskey was $1.25 a bottle while brandy and rum went for $4.50 per bottle. Soldiers, however, were quite ingenious about procuring and hiding liquor. One officer, puzzled by his men's ability to conceal the liquor with which they were constantly becoming drunk, was amazed to discover that they had stopped up the touch-holes of their muskets with slivers of wood and then filled the barrels with whiskey, taking care always to carry the weapons muzzle upward. The issue and sale of alcohol to the troops was deplored by many officers because it could, in the words of Alexander McMullen lead to a "scene of dissipation". The practise continued, however, throughout the war.[23]

Drunkenness was often a cause of breaches of the strict discipline of the wartime army. For those found guilty, there were harsh punishments although they did not include flogging, which had been abolished just before the outbreak of war.[24] Other, perhaps more cruel, methods were instead used: "running the gauntlet", picketing (standing with one bare foot on a sharpened stake), branding, the wearing of a ball and chain, confinement to a "black hole", and, finally, execution by hanging or firing squad. At first used sparingly (only three soldiers were executed in 1812), by the later war years, the supreme penalty became almost common — 146 men were executed in 1814. In all, 260 American soldiers were sentenced to death during the War of 1812 and 205 actually suffered the sentence.[25]

Execution was most commonly used to punish the crime of desertion. And desertion was a major problem — it has been estimated that 12.7% of those who enlisted, deserted one or more times during the war, and that, overall, the army lost 10.1% of its total strength through desertion. In December 1812 and again in July 1814, the government was forced to issue blanket pardons to get men back into the ranks. The problem seems to have been more prevalent during the last year of the war, perhaps brought on by the increased recruiting bounties paid for enlistment and muster.

Drummer Hanks believed that men deserted to escape "despotic officers", to free themselves from "military bondage", from homesickness or because

---

[23] Alcohol ration from *1812 Regulations*, p. 52; General Order, Camp Meigs, April 21, 1813, in Lindley, *Fort Meigs*, p. 11; Fredriksen, "Chronicle of Valour", p. 243.

[24] Prior to May 1812, under Article 87 of the Articles of War, offenders could be punished by up to fifty lashes, but under "An Act making further Provisions for the Army of the United States", approved May 16, 1812, "the infliction of corporal punishment, by stripes or lashes" was repealed. See *1812 Regulations*, pp. 32, 94.

[25] On military punishments and the figures for execution, see John S. Hare, "Military Punishments in the War of 1812", *Journal of the American Military Institute*, IV (1940), pp. 225-39.

they were "fickle-minded". Colonel James Welborn of the 10th Infantry, on the other hand, believed that men deserted because "their rights were not attended to."[26] Certainly the government often neglected the wants of the soldiers — in May 1815 a near mutiny occurred in the 3rd Rifle Regiment at Buffalo because the enlisted men of the unit had received neither their enlistment bonus nor the ten months pay owed to them.[27]

If daily life was hard enough for the enlisted man in camp, it was doubly so in the field. Consider the perils of combat. From July to October 1814, the men of the Left Division fought two pitched battles (Chippawa and Lundy's Lane), one siege (Fort Erie) and almost daily minor actions and skirmishes. They paid a high price: the official casualty returns for the major actions alone of the campaign totalled 1,824 men. But there was a worse peril — illness. More American soldiers died from sickness during the war than from enemy bullets (8.2% of the total number as opposed to the 3.2% of the total who were killed in action). Given the sanitary standards of the time, the Niagara area, with its hot, humid summers and cold, wet winters was an unhealthy place. Ford and Hanks avoided illness but McMullen spent his last month in service as an invalid suffering from one of the many varieties of fever that afflicted the men of the division.[28]

---

[26] Sara McCullough Lemon, *Frustrated Patriots: North Carolina and the War of 1812* (Chapel Hill, 1975), pp. 51-52.

[27] Wartime desertion statistics from Stagg, "Enlisted Men", p. 624; information on pardons and account of the near-mutiny at Buffalo in 1815 from Lemon, *Frustrated Patriots,* pp. 53-55.

In fairness to the American army, it should be noted that desertion was also a problem in the British army. The six British regiments that fought against the Left Division in the summer of 1814 lost 211 men from desertion between January and June of that year. See Great Britain, Public Record Office, War Office 17, Returns of the Army, vols. 1516-1518. During the siege of Fort Erie in August-September 1814, 113 British and Canadian soldiers deserted to the enemy. See Register of Deserters from the Enemy, National Archives, Record Group 98, Quartermaster File, Left Division, reproduced in Whitehorne, *While Washington Burned,* p. 187, Annex R. The inescapable conclusion is that military service was not popular with the men of any nationality.

[28] Casualty statistics for the Left Division from Cruikshank, *Documentary History,* I: p. 43, Report of the Killed and Wounded of the Left Division, July 5, 1814; p. 121, Morgan to Brown, August 5, 1814; p. 150, Report of the Killed and Wounded during the Cannonading and the Bombardment, August 15, 1814 and Report of the Killed, Wounded and Missing of the Left Division, August 15, 1814; p. 214, Report of the Killed, Wounded & Missing [during the sortie of September 17, 1814]; Vol. II, pp. 420-23, Report of the Killed, Wounded & Missing, July 25, 1814.

These are the "official" casualty returns, but it should be noted that recent research indicates that many of the numbers in these returns, which were compiled immediately after the action, appear to be too high. See, for example, the casualty lists for the siege of Fort Erie in Whitehorne, *While Washington Burned,* Annexes J to N.

General statistics for wartime deaths from disease and enemy action from Stagg, "Enlisted Men", p. 624.

Despite all the rigors and hardships of military life, the men of the Left Division performed superbly in 1814. They did so for a variety of reasons. One pertained to the nature of the United States Army as a whole. Despite all its difficulties in recruiting and training, the infantry regiments of the regular army enjoyed a strong asset in that they were largely recruited from a particular state or region. Thus, Drummer Hanks's 11th Infantry was primarily a Vermont unit, nearly two-thirds of the officers and men coming from that state, while Ford's 23rd Infantry was primarily a New York unit. Citizen soldier McMullen was fortunate to serve in a company of volunteers from his home county in Pennsylvania. The regional affiliation and ties of such units gave them a group cohesion that contributed to their ability to perform under stress.[29]

More particularly, the Left Division possessed a number of special attributes that rendered it unique. Its senior officers, Brown, Scott, Ripley and Porter, were men of proven ability who had seen considerable combat on the frontier during the war. The quality of the junior officers and enlisted men was also good, most being veterans of two major campaigns in the north. The division was trained intensively, and trained well, prior to taking the field. Most important, perhaps, it was trained, or forged, by the same men who led it into combat — officers and men knew each other and both knew what was expected. Finally, the division was victorious in its first major engagement — the battle of Chippawa, 5 July 1814 — a tremendous boost to its morale.

Major General Jacob Brown's Left Division was the most professional and effective military organization fielded by the United States in 1812-1815. At least, its enemy thought so — one British officer commenting on the Niagara campaign noted that it was "but justice to the American soldier to observe that he seems to have wonderfully improved in the last year of the war."[30]

But it is now time to listen to the words of three members of that distinguished formation — a 14-year-old drummer boy from Vermont, an 18-year-old private from New York, and a 23-year old militiaman from Pennsylvania.

Donald E. Graves
Almonte, Ontario

---

[29] On the 11th Infantry and its officers, see E.P. Walton (ed.), *Records of the Governor and Council of the State of Vermont*, Vol. VI (Montpelier, 1878), p. 474. On the regional affiliations of the other units, see the text below and Whitehorne, *While Washington Burned*, Annex C.

[30] James Carmichael-Smyth, *Precis of the Wars in Canada* (London, 1862), p. 193.

Editor's Note

Major editorial work on the following memoirs was restricted to dividing the memoirs into titled sections for ease of reference. In some cases, new paragraphing was introduced to break up the density of 19th century prose and to give the narrative better movement. Major errors or inconsistencies in fact have been indicated in the notes while simple errors in dates and the spelling of proper and place names have been silently corrected. For consistency, the modern spelling of Sackets Harbor and Chippawa has been used throughout the text. Period spelling and capitalization, ampersands and "&c." have been kept for flavor, but superscripts have been omitted. None of these minor editorial functions have altered the original texts in any substantial way.

The text notes, which are intended to clarify and complement the memoirs, provide additional information on the persons, place and events mentioned in the main text. Although every reasonable effort was made to make these notes as complete as possible, where no such identification is contained in a note, either insufficient direction was given in the main text to find the relevant information, or it was not available.

... D.G.

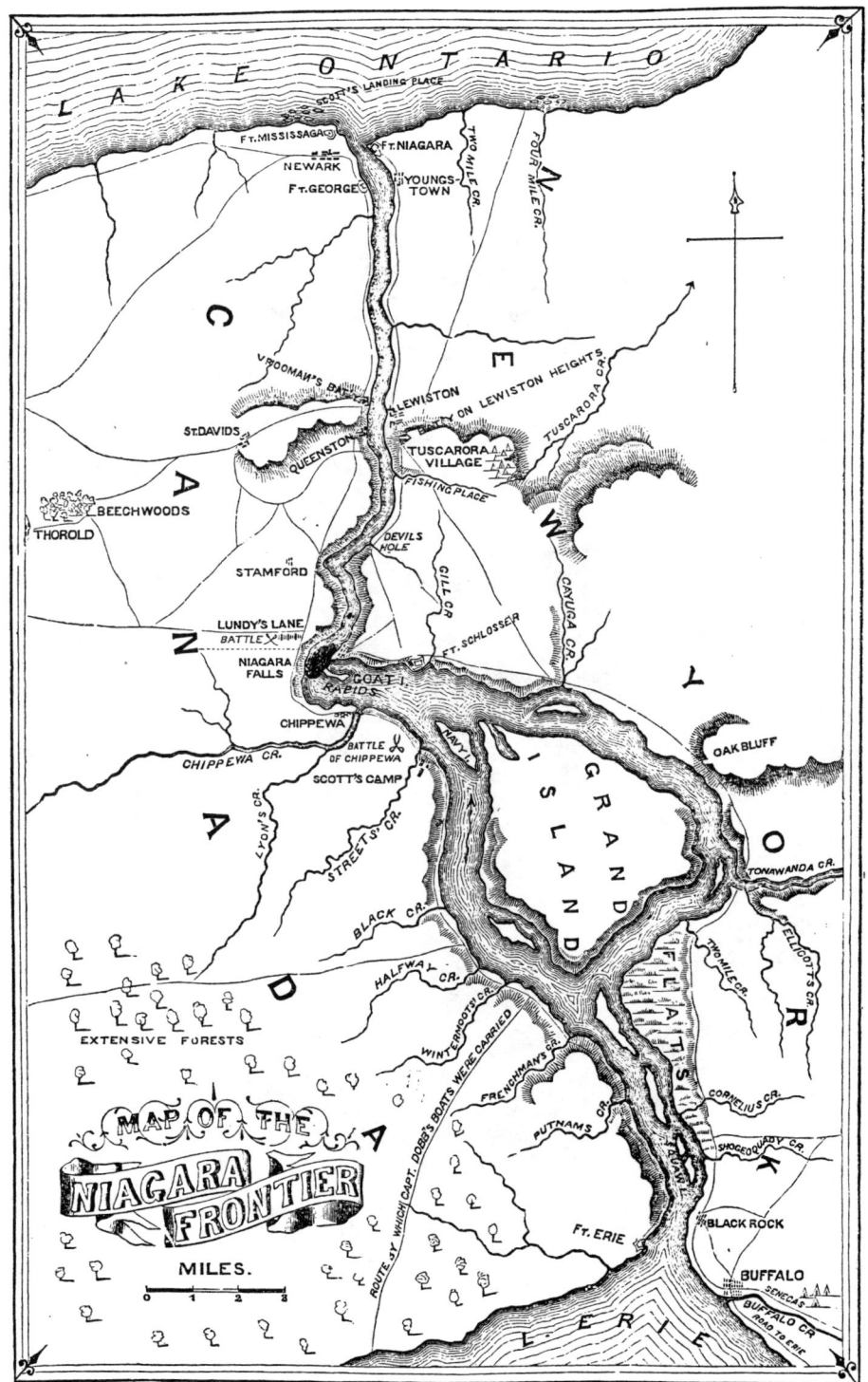

From Benson J. Lossing's *Pictorial Field Book of the War of 1812.*

Drummer Jarvis HANKS
11th U.S. Infantry

I.

The Memoir of
Drummer Jarvis Frary Hanks,

11th Infantry,

1813-1815

The following pages of my biography are recorded for my own amusement, and for the perusal of a few friends. They have filled up my leisure hours, perhaps not unprofitably, and may yet serve a good purpose in the review of them, and show me all the way of life in which kind Providence has led me. I have written more familiarly, and with less reserve, because I would be reminded of the minutiae of God's dealings; therefore, hairbreadth escapes in battles, almost fatal accidents, preservation from open vice and capital sins, will be noticed. And God grant that a review of these may lead me to repentance and greater measure of faith in the Lord Jesus Christ, to honour my Creator and Preserver, in my life, health, influence, reason, and all that I have and am.

New York City, January 1831
Jarvis Frary Hanks

1. Early Life and Decision to Enlist

I was born in Pittsford, Otsego County, New York, on the 24th of September 1799. I am the son of Joseph Hanks, whose father's name was William, who lived in the green mountains of Vermont, and whose progenitors emigrated from Holland. It is not improbable that our name was once called *Von Hankstad*, but has been fully anglicised in its way down to the present time. My Mother's maiden name was Anna Frary and her descent is traced to *"the pilgrims"*.

In 1801 my father removed to Pawlet, Vt. where he resided till 1817. I was sent to a common country school, at the age of four years, and at eleven, had made considerable progress in the elements of an English education. I evinced at an early age, an attachment to music, not commonly found among children. In my eighth year I committed the rudiments to memory, under the tuition of Benoni Adams, and for a number of years made some advances in the science.

In 1810, on account of my repeated solicitations, and most likely because my kind father was willing to indulge my wishes, he consented and I was removed to an adjoining town, where I learned to beat the drum. The reason of my choice of this in preference to another instrument were: I thought it produced the most pleasing noise; I knew that the drummer occupied a conspicuous station in the ranks of a regiment, and that a boy not older than myself, being a good performer, was looked on as a prodigy. The exercise required and the activity of the arms which might be displayed, by an adept, were inducements too powerful for me, at that age, to resist. In consequence of this, I now see that I was prepared to enter the army, in the service of my country, as a musician; which actually took place three years afterwards; whereas I could not have rendered the least service under arms, at so tender an age as that of fourteen years.

At this period, likewise, I was pleased with painting, and thought I should like to make it a business for life. I visited my uncle's shop in the vicinity, frequently, and was not an indolent observer of what transpired there. David Frary, brother of my mother, was this uncle of whom I speak. He was a joiner[31] and a carpenter, and was also in the practice of painting houses, wagons, chairs, etc. From him I learned the due proportion in the mixture of paints, and the pigments employed in each colour. He encouraged my taste and did what he could to forward and instruct me. I soon became somewhat proficient in ornamental work, so that in about a year from that time I painted many of his small jobs in quite handsome style.

In 1813, my mind became unsettled, and I entertained a thousand notions concerning my future life, and endeavoured to think of something new, and at the same time profitable and pleasing. Having fluctuated long, and yet remaining undecided, my father being unwilling to interfere with my inclinations, an incident occurred, which brought me to a determination, at least, for the present. A sergeant of the United States Army, under the authority of the government, made his appearance in Pawlet, beating up for recruits, offering twenty dollars bounty (advance pay) and *160 acres of land,* to any who would enlist for either five years, or during the war. My youthful mind was fired with ardor in anticipation of a soldier's career; the pomp and splendour of a military life were vividly portrayed in my foolish imagination, and produced a desire to engage in the service, which was not to be relinquished. I enlisted, as a drummer, with my father's consent, for the term of the continuance of the war and was charged to appear in Rutland, the rendezvous, within the ten days following.

---

[31] A "joiner" is a craftsman who makes furniture, household fittings and other fine woodwork.

Several items here demand particular remark:

1. I wanted only a few months of fourteen years of age, and yet, young as I was, the officer had no objection to me as a musician; nay, he seemed quite desirous of securing me. Probably he would have refused to give me a place in the ranks as a private, under the burthens of a heavy musket.

2. My father consented to abandon me to the vicissitudes, and vices, and dangers of a life of war, for an uncertain length of time; it might be only a few months, or it might continue for many years. I should be set afloat, without a friend or guardian, to guide or protect me; to counsel or reprove; should be exposed to a thousand temptations, some of which, perhaps, might prove my ruin. I might be sick, some of the loathsome diseases of the camp might prey upon my vitals, and, what was more likely, the ball or bayonet of an enemy, might pierce my heart and sink me to a premature grave. If these evils were escaped, intemperance might make me her slave and degrade me to the level of a brute. I do not know whether these thoughts occurred to him, on consenting to my absence, or not, but I am fully persuaded that considerations like these should have determined him peremptorily to refuse; and however I may differ with him in opinion, I conceive it was his duty to dissuade me from my purpose by all the arguments of parental affection and the restraints of parental authority.

3. Providence evidently directed the decision relating to my term of enlistment. In consequence of some unaccounted impression, we were induced to choose "*during the war*", in preference to "*five years*", which proved to be only twenty-six months.

The most trying scene I had ever passed thro' was now to be experienced. I was about to leave the home and companions of my childhood — to bid farewell to those who had been reared at the same boards and to whose wants the same kind maternal hand had ministered — to those who gave me life, and provided for all my necessities and I might never return. The thought came over me like the winds of autumn, with a gloomy solemnity. My excellent and affectionate mother had hitherto concealed her anxiety for my welfare, and the pain she felt in anticipation of her bereavement in the loss of her oldest son; for she has since informed me that she would rather have seen me decently buried than go into the army. She looked forward with a mother's solicitude to the various dangers of the battle field; the fatigues of wearisome journeying; the

"The most trying scene I ever passed through..."

influence of abandoned associates, and a thousand nameless evils, which pressed upon her wounded heart with an overwhelming weight. When previously consulted by my father concerning my enlistment, she remonstrated but to no purpose. And now it was too late! for the fatal instrument had been executed, whose conditions require one to serve my country so long as the war should continue, and that act could not be recalled.

I took an affectionate leave of the family, and lastly, of my mother. She grasped my hand in such a manner as conveyed the agony of her inmost soul. Her eyes were overflowed with tears, and raised to Heaven. I can never forget her explanation at that moment — it was one of deep sorrow mingled with patient submission. She seemed to say, though she spoke not, — "Thy will be done, O Lord — Onto thy protection, God of hope and mercy, I resign my boy! Let it please Thee to spare him, that thy handmaid may see his face again in the land of the living — prepare him for all the events of thy Providence, and save his soul from everlasting ruin." I gently withdrew my hand and made haste to depart. Her prayers were heard & answered in my preservation and return to her embraces.

2. First Months in the Army

My father accompanied me to Wells, a village four miles from his residence, where we dined. He also purchased and presented me a small book, which contained a variety of maxims and miscellaneous observations on morals and religion peculiarly adapted to my capacity and age. It was done in a manner calculated to impress on my mind, a strict observance of the rules therein contained. We separated after exchanging our mutual promise of correspondence during my absence from home.

I now made my way to Rutland, the headquarters for recruits enlisted by Sergeant Sanford. Here I found ninety men who had enlisted as privates. We were placed under the command of Captain Gordon[32] of the 11th Regt. U.S. Infantry. On the 20th of April, we marched for Burlington, and arrived in four or five days, during which I had a slight foretaste of the fare I was to enjoy in future. Now was the first time I had ever slept on any thing harder than feathers, neither had I eaten any kind of meat unless it was previously well cooked. I now devoured raw pork with greediness and was obliged to sleep, sometimes on hay in a barn, and sometimes on the "*soft side of a pine board*", as we used to say. I submitted to these inconveniences without murmuring; but was sorry enough that, for these, I had exchanged the comforts of my mother's cupboard. I

---

[32] Captain Samuel Gordon, 11th Infantry, a native of Vermont.

endeavoured to keep up a good flow of spirits, not by "*pouring down spirits*" which I had in possession, but by associating with the most loquacious of my comrades. The pleasures of friendly converse soon diverted my mind from the present trouble of marching and privations, & I anticipated better times when we should arrive at our place of destination.

Let it here be remarked that the officer who enlisted me, as an additional inducement, promised I should not be compelled to go into battle but should be retained in the recruiting service and remain at Burlington or its vicinity. The sequel will prove that no regard was paid to this engagement, and probably he never thought of it again, after he had accomplished his purpose.

When we arrived at camp, our provisions were exhausted, our feet blistered, our spirits low and dejected. We were met three miles out by a detachment of men, who escorted us to the barracks where we were to be quartered. It was on Sunday; my surprise was great, when I found no special regard was paid to this sacred day in the cantonment. I had always been accustomed to attend public worship on every Sabbath while at home and I was at a loss how to spend it otherwise now. Shortly, however, I could waste and profane that day with as little compunction of conscience as any of those whose evil example so readily influenced my unguarded heart to consent to such disregard of the Command of God.

I had not been here long, when I witnessed an awful punishment, inflicted on a soldier, for the crime of desertion. His sentence was to have one hundred stripes on his back by the method styled "*running the gauntlet*", and then to wear a ball & chain at hard labour, for the term of five years. I will describe these punishments in detail, as well to show their influence in restraining me from committing the same crime, as well as what evils are brought upon men, in consequence of wars — what miseries follow the exercise of the baser passions of the human heart. If the precepts of Christ were universally obeyed, it would be impossible to produce war.

Two ranks of men (fifty in each) facing inwards, struck the offender one stroke on his naked back, with a green switch, as he passed along, between them. Soldiers, with bayonets pointed at him preceded and followed so that the poor wretch could neither run nor escape, but was compelled to bear his torture without remedy. The blood ran down his back in streams, which was entirely divested of its integuments and presented a spectacle to melt the heart of a stone. A cannon ball, weighing twenty-four pounds, was attached to his ankle by an iron chain about eight or ten feet in length, & he [was] removed to the guard house, to be in readiness to commence his five years' task.[33]

---

[33] Jarvis Hanks served at Burlington under the command of Major General Wade Hampton, a strict, almost cruel, disciplinarian. For a record of the daily camp life at Burlington in 1813, see "Garrison Orders, Burlington, Vermont, July 13-August 4, 1813", *Moorsfield Antiquarian*, I (1937), pp. 79-103.

After remaining two months at Burlington, we were ordered to Sackets Harbor, a military post on Lake Ontario. We embarked on a steam boat, (I believe the first one ever built on Champlain) and landed at Whitehall. From thence our way lay through Glenn's Falls, Jessup's Landing, Johnstown, Newport and Rome, to the place of destination. At a small town in Montgomery County, the people came with wagon loads of potatoes, milk, and other good things, which they presented to our officers to be served out to the soldiers, as a testimony of their hearty welcome they gave us, and of their disposition to forward us on towards the frontiers, where the enemy were daily expected.

It was a scene of great interest to witness the violent destruction of life for the crime of desertion. Various reasons induced the soldiers clandestinely to leave the army. In some instances they fled to escape the despotic and brutal treatment of a superior; in others, to free themselves from military bondage in its ordinary form. Some could not endure longer absence from relatives and friends; others, naturally unsteady and fickle minded, sought the gratification of their ruling passion in a constant change of locality and circumstance. But scarcely *any* finally escaped. An argus-eyed police searched out the place of their retreat, and dragged them back, with disgrace to the camp. The punishment for desertion is *death,* generally. If any other be substituted, it is only in cases where the delinquent is very young, or some other redeeming circumstance mitigates the nature of the offence.[34]

Two men were hung at this post in June, a few days after our arrival. They were both placed on the gallows together. When the executioner cut the rope which held the drop, they both fell, one to rise no more, the other, to the ground. The rope broke above his head. He seemed but little hurt. He stood upon his feet, on terra-firma, while his companion swung in view, struggling in the agonies of death.

A deep groan of horror burst involuntarily from the surrounding thousands of their fellows in arms who had been drawn up to witness the wages of insubordination. They hoped, however, that the living man would now be pardoned, as Providence seemed to have so signally interposed in his behalf. But our hopes were disappointed. At the command of an officer, Jack Ketch[35] tied the fatal knot around the miserable fellow's throat, threw the other end of it over the top of the gallows, and with the assistance of another or two persons, drew him up high enough to choke him to death. We were compelled to

---

[34] For an account of the problem of desertion in the wartime United States Army and the disciplinary measures taken to counter it, see Hare, "Military Punishments", pp. 225-39.

[35] "Jack Ketch" was period slang for a hangman.

remain upon the ground until life was extinct, a period of twenty or thirty minutes.

The custom of inflicting the punishment of death by hanging or shooting has universally prevailed in the army of the United States for the crime of desertion, except in cases of extreme youth, aberration of mind, old age, &c. In these, wearing the ball and chain, expelling from camp and from the army, with a straw halter round the neck, shaving half the hair from the head, branding the cheek with the infamous letter "D" and an escort of musicians playing the Rogue's March,[36] are many times substituted.

A short time only elapsed until we were again drawn up in a hollow square around a gallows to see a deserter hung. He was a youth of about the age of sixteen years, and had deserted four times, and seemed determined to effect his final escape or die in the attempt. For the first three crimes he was successively and generously pardoned on account of his infancy. But his fourth could not be suffered to pass unpunished. A short prayer was offered up to the throne of grace by the Chaplain, and the unhappy young man was launched into eternity.

3. The Campaign on the St. Lawrence, 1813-1814

Our regiment, with several others, remained here until October when we all embarked, in open boats, on Lake Ontario for Grenadier Island, which lies at the point where the lake empties itself into the St. Lawrence River. On this Island, about eight thousand troops were concentrated, preparatory to making a descent upon Montreal, under command of Gen[era]l Wilkinson.[37]

I must here relate a little anecdote to illustrate the character of the American soldiers, and show how covetous men, like the dog and the shadow in the fable, in seeking to grasp too much, may lose all. Grenadier Island is several miles in extent, and contains many farms well cultivated. It is much nearer to Kingston, a British garrison, in Canada than to Sackets Harbor, an American post; and yet it belongs to the United States. One farmer, near our encampment, had still

---

[36] A tradition inherited from the British army, the "drumming out" of a miscreant soldier had been practiced in that service from the early eighteenth century. The traditional "Rogue's March" tune dates from the mid part of that century, and British soldiers added these words:

> *Fifty I got for selling my coat,*
> *Fifty for selling my blanket,*
> *If ever I 'list for a soldier again,*
> *The devil shall be my sergeant.*

See Lewis Winstock, *Songs and Music of the Redcoats, 1642-1902* (London, 1970), pp. 96-97.

[37] Major General James Wilkinson (1767-1825). A distinguished veteran of the Revolutionary War whose later career never lived up to its early promise, Wilkinson was court martialed for his actions during the campaign of 1813. He was acquitted and later honorably discharged.

in the ground a number of hundreds of bushels of potatoes. Soldiers are not generally very conscientious about appropriating to their own use almost any thing that comes in their way, especially eatables, if they are hungry. With regards, however, to these potatoes, the owner was offered fifty cents a bushel for them, if he would dispose of as many as were wanted for that price. In refusing this proposition, he added, with an air of triumph, and self complacence, that he "could get a dollar a bushel for them in Kingston".

It was soon noised around in the Camp that an American farmer was intending to supply provisions to the enemies against whom we were contending and before the next morning, it was decided that he would be saved the trouble and expense of digging his potatoes, and of transporting them to market. The Soldiers had relieved him of the burden, and when he applied to the officers to remunerate him for his loss, they gave him no encouragement, or consolation, in the premises, and he retired, lamenting his unwise decision, which had resulted so unfortunately for him.[38]

In the first days of November, Gen[era]l Wilkinson being prepared, the army embarked in batteaux, and small boats, and set out for Montreal. We passed the Thousand islands, the "Long Sault", (pronounced "Sew") and Ogdensburg, a village in St. Lawrence County, N.Y., opposite Prescott in Canada. Here most of the soldiers disembarked, about a mile above, and remained till midnight, when, after building large fires, they marched down the American shore three or four miles, while the boats, with muffled oars, were rowed as silently as possible, past Prescott. The British, however, fired several cannon shot at them and killed and wounded several men. Otherwise, however, but little injury was sustained.

The army again embarked and passed on down to Williamsburg, or "Chrysler's field"[39] on the Canadian side. We arrived here on the 10th of November and went ashore, built fires of the rail fences. It was very cold, raining and sleeting all night. I remember well that I had at that time a leather cap, and kept it on my head while I slept. Before morning I had, in trying to keep warm, changed my position with relation to the fire, and placed both my head and feet in such close contact with it repeatedly, that my cap and shoes were burnt so badly as to be nearly valueless. I was soon supplied with others in their place, and was comfortable again.

---

[38] Hanks does not exaggerate when he states that American farmers were willing to sell their produce to the enemy. In the spring of 1813, Surgeon William Dunlop of the British army was dining at Cornwall with the local commander when their meal was interrupted by an American from Vermont offering to sell one hundred head of cattle he had crossed over at St. Regis and driven to their very door. See William Dunlop, *Tiger Dunlop's Upper Canada* (Toronto, 1967), pp. 22-23.

[39] Actually John Crysler's field, or farm, where the battle was fought on November 11, 1813 was a few miles from the Canadian hamlet of Williamsburg.

On the 11th the battle was fought at this place. It commenced about 10 A.M. and continued until 4 P.M., six hours, when we retreated to our boats and rowed down a few miles and landed on the American shore and camped for the night. In this battle we lost Gen[era]l Covington[40] and several other officers, and some two hundred men killed and wounded; but it is difficult to say which had the advantage, on the whole.[41]

After this we passed St. Regis, an Indian village on the New York side, and soon entered the Salmon River, and proceeded up nine miles, to "French Mills".[42] Winter had now set in, and being in forty-five degrees N[orth]. Latitude there was no hope of being able to prosecute the campaign further and we took up our winter quarters in this dreary and desolate spot.

We pitched our tents, spread hemlock boughs for our beds, built temporary fire-places of stones and clay mortar and made ourselves as comfortable as he nature of the case would admit. The snow was soon four feet deep and the cold excessive. By the middle of January the barracks were completed, and we commenced occupying them. The first job of *tailoring* I ever performed, was here. I had two blankets, and cut and made a pair of pantaloons out of one of them; as I needed the latter article much more than the former. Oh! what a pair of breeches!

4. Scott's Camp at Buffalo

After remaining in our barracks till about the middle of February 1814, we were ordered to march to Buffalo, so as to be ready for the campaign in that quarter early in the summer. We burnt the barracks, the boats which transported us there, which were frozen up in the river, and several hundred barrels of provisions, mostly flour, which we had no means of removing, and which it was determined should not fall into the hands of the enemy. We commenced our march by the light of as fine a conflagration as has been seen

---

[40] Brigadier General Leonard Covington (1768-1813). A professional soldier, Covington had fought with Anthony Wayne against the northwest Indian confederacy in the 1790s before resigning to pursue a career in politics. He rejoined the army in 1809 as a colonel of light dragoons.

[41] Although losses were heavy on both sides, there is no doubt that Crysler's Farm was a British victory. Outnumbered two to one, the British commander, Lieutenant Colonel Joseph Morrison, picked a good defensive position on the banks of the St. Lawrence River and repulsed a series of uncoordinated attacks by the larger American force. The official American casualties reported for this action were more than four hundred killed, wounded and captured. British casualties numbered 179. For an account of the battle see Ronald Way, "The Day of Crysler's Farm", *Canadian Geographical Journal*, LXII (1961), pp. 184-217.

[42] Present day Fort Covington, New York.

in modern times; and through snow and mud, "o'er hill & dale", sometimes on foot and sometimes in pressed sleighs and wagons, after much fatigue and weariness we arrived at our place of destination some time in April.[43]

The winter previous the town was burned by the British and Indians, and only one house was left on the ground, in a condition to be occupied, and that, if I remember right, was the property of a widow woman. When we came there, & saw the smouldering ruins, it gave us feelings of deep sympathy for the desolate and plundered inhabitants; and sharpened up our courage to prepare for effectual retaliation when we should enter Canada upon the anticipated campaign.[44]

The site of Buffalo was extremely beautiful, gently sloping towards the North West, and commanding an extensive prospect of the lake and adjacent country. We continued here until July, under of the command of Major Gen[era]l. Jacob Brown.[45] We were drilled daily in the most systematic manner. In the morning after breakfast, every sergeant exercised his squad of from twelve to twenty men, in the various evolutions, for one hour. Captains drilled their companies from 11 to 12. And at 1 or 2 o'clock P.M., the whole brigade, with all its officers, musicians and privates, under the command of Gen. Winfield Scott,[46] the most thorough disciplinarian I ever saw, were

---

[43] Hanks is compressing events here. Major General Jacob Brown was actually ordered to march to Sackets Harbor with a brigade of infantry plus additional artillery and cavalry units. He arrived in early February 1814 to find ambiguous orders from Secretary of War John Armstrong. After much puzzlement, Brown decided to march to Buffalo where he arrived early in April.

[44] This is an exaggeration. Buffalo was burned by the British late in December 1813 in retaliation for the needless American destruction of the Canadian village of Newark (today Niagara-on-the-Lake, Ontario). The ruins were cold by the time Jarvis arrived on the scene.

[45] Major General Jacob Brown (1775-1828). A prewar landowner from Jefferson County, Brown was responsible for opening up the Black River country of northern New York. A general in the state militia at the outbreak of war, his prominent role in the successful defense of both Ogdensburg and Sackets Harbor against British attacks brought him a regular army commission as a brigadier general. He performed well during the ill-fated 1813 campaign and was promoted to major general and given command of the Left Division. Jacob Brown fought and won more battles against British regular troops than any other American general of either the War of 1812 or the Revolutionary War. He was general-in-chief of the postwar army and instrumental in increasing the professionalism of that service.

[46] Brigadier General Winfield Scott (1786-1866). A prewar regular officer, Scott gained rapid promotion to the rank of brigadier general in the spring of 1814 following a dazzling series of successes. Aggressive and obstinate, Scott was a firm believer in properly preparing his troops for battle. For a ten-week period at Buffalo in the spring of 1814, he conducted the most effective training camp the United States army was to experience during the war. For a recent examination of his training activities at Buffalo in the spring of 1814, see Donald E. Graves, "'I have a handsome little army': A Re-examination of Winfield Scott's Camp at Buffalo in 1814", in R. Arthur Bowler (ed.), *War Along the Niagara: Essays on the War of 1812 and Its Legacy* (Youngstown, NY, 1991), pp. 43-52.

"The most thorough disciplinarian I ever saw..."

drilled from three to four hours. These exercises, continued daily, for more than two months, could not fail to make us well acquainted with our business as soldiers and fit us for the contests which were expected during the summer in the enemy's country.[47]

During the time we remained at Buffalo, five men were sentenced to be publicly shot for the offense of desertion. They were dressed in white robes with white caps upon their heads, and a red target fastened over the heart. The army was drawn up into a hollow square to witness the example that was about to be made of their comrades who had proved recreant to the regulations of the service. Five graves were dug in a row, five coffins placed near them, also in a line, with distance between coffins and graves, to enable the criminals to kneel between them. About twelve men were assigned to the execution of each offender. Their guns were loaded by officers, and they were not permitted to examine them afterwards until they had fired.

All things being in readiness, the chaplain made a prayer, the caps were pulled down over the eyes of the poor culprits, and the word of command given: "Ready! Aim! Fire!" They all fell! Some into their graves, some over their coffins. One struggled faintly and the commanding officer ordered a sergeant to approach and end his misery. He obeyed by putting the muzzle of his piece within a yard of his head, and discharging it. This quieted him perfectly!

At this time one of the condemned slowly arose from his recumbent position to his knees and was assisted to his feet. His first remark was, "By G__, I thought I was dead". In consequence of his youth and the peculiar circumstances of his case, he had been reprieved, but the fact was not communicated to him, until this moment. He had anticipated execution with his comrades, and when the report of the guns took place, he fell with them, though not a ball touched him. The platoon assigned to him, had guns given to them which were not charged, or at least had nothing but powder in them.

This young soldier was only eighteen years of age and had been recently transferred to Captain Bliss's[48] company. This officer was a cruel, tyrannical man, and the soldiers all hated him most cordially. As this youthful son of Mars was permitted to return to his quarters accompanied by many of his fellows, he remarked that he would desert again, if obliged to remain under the command of Capt. Bliss. He was soon suffered to resume his place in the company to

---

[47] Scott took a highly personal interest in the training of his troops. Captain John Murdock of the 25th Infantry, whose unit was at the Buffalo camp, wrote that "General Scott drills & damns, drills & damns, and drills again." See Murdock to Gardner, May 26, 1814, Gardner Papers, New York State Library, Albany.

[48] Captain John Bliss, 11th Infantry. A native of New Hampshire, Bliss was wounded at the battle of Lundy's Lane, July 25, 1814.

which he originally belonged, where he was well satisfied, and exhibited no further disposition to insubordination.[49]

Before we crossed over into Canada, we were all furnished with a grey suit of clothes, consisting of a *round-about*, or sailor's jacket, and pantaloons. This was done to deceive the enemy and lead him to suppose we were *"militia"*, instead of *"regulars"*.[50]

5. The Campaign on the Niagara: Chippawa and Lundy's Lane

On the 3rd of July, we were conveyed in boats at 2 o'clock at night, over the Niagara river, opposite Black Rock, a mile or two below Fort Erie, which was then in the keeping of about ninety British soldiers. We remained in front of the fort during the day, and at about sundown, the Fort was surrendered into our hands, without any bloodshed. The prisoners of war were immediately sent to Buffalo.

On the 4th we marched down the river to the plains of Chippawa, about three miles above the fort,[51] and made our encampment. Meantime a hasty fortification was thrown up during the night, in which our cannon were planted.

On the 5th our picket guards were several times driven in by the Indians and the enemy's pickets, who were sheltered from our fire by a dense wood. At 5 o'clock, the whole force of Chippawa was discovered advancing upon our position, with evident intention of giving us battle. Our army was in readiness, and in a few moments were marching in solid column to meet them.

We were compelled to pass a narrow bridge over a creek,[52] near where our artillery was stationed. The enemy here had as favorable an opportunity of cutting us all to pieces as they could desire; but their balls and grape, mostly passed over our heads, and fell into a bend of the river where they glanced along for some distance upon its surface and then sunk to the bottom without having done any damage. A few men, however, were killed in passing this bridge.

---

[49] The young soldier was private William Fairfield, 11th Infantry. See General Order, Buffalo, June 3, 1814, Left Division Order Book, New York State Library.

[50] Although the issue of grey uniforms to the soldiers of Scott's brigade did, in the end, confuse the British, it was not deliberately intended to do so. Scott indented for the regulation blue coatees or short-tailed coats for his men from the quartermaster but received instead short, tail-less jackets normally worn as an undergarment in winter. These he issued to his troops. See Chartrand, *Uniforms and Equipment,* pp. 43-44.

[51] Hanks is referring here to the fortified village of Chippawa, not Fort Erie.

[52] In 1814 this was called Street's Creek. It is now known as Ussher's Creek.

Soon we were formed into line, though under the enemy's fire, in a meadow, where the grass was about three feet high and very thrifty. The firing continued on both sides without the least cessation, or the least distraction, in either army, for 75 or 80 minutes, when the British soldiers and officers, who had been victorious at Waterloo, under Field Marshal Wellington, and under other commanders on different occasions in various parts of Europe, turned their backs upon the grey-coated American Militia, as they supposed we were, and fled in terror and precipitation to their fortress.[53] We, of course, gave them chase but they took the precaution to cut away the bridge over the Chippawa river, so as to prevent the possibility of our reaching them at that time.[54]

During this battle, Sergeant Eliah T. Bond stood still, in one spot, and fired sixteen cartridges, while I stood by his side, with my drum slung over my shoulder, and held his ramrod, instead of his putting it into his gun, when he fired, as is customary among all soldiers. By this manoeuvre, considerable time was saved, and he [was] enabled to fire a number more bullets than he could otherwise have done.

In two or three days the enemy evacuated Chippawa and retreated to Fort George. We constructed a floating bridge and followed them, remaining a few days at Queenston.

Here, with other soldier boys, I went into the Niagara river to bathe, daily, and sometimes oftener. I suppose the water fifteen or twenty feet in depth, at the wharves, near the warehouses. Before I left home, I had been accustomed to jump off the bridge into the mill pond near my father's house probably twelve feet high. At Queenston, I habituated myself to jump out of the third storey of a warehouse, which was twenty-five or thirty feet above the water, and over a wharf of twelve feet in width. It is surprising that I was not killed or drowned; but it is really true that I escaped without the slightest injury. Let it be remembered that this was twenty years before Sam Patch flourished.[55]

At Fort George we only remained a single day.[56] I saw Gen[era]l Scott and several of his officers reconnoitring the fort with telescopes, while the enemy

---

[53] Hanks refers again to the fortified village of Chippawa. In point of fact, with the exception of some of the officers, none of the British regulars in General Phineas Riall's force were veterans of Wellington's army. The battle of Waterloo was not fought until June 1815.

[54] The British army suffered close to two hundred casualties of all types at Chippawa. The American army reported 182 casualties of all types. For an account of this action, see Donald E. Graves, *Red Coats and Grey Jackets: The Battle of Chippawa, 5 July 1814* (Toronto, 1994).

[55] During the 1830s, Sam Patch thrilled crowds with feats of daredevil diving.

[56] Brown's army actually lay before Fort George for two days — July 20 and 21, 1814.

lay about a mile distant. The enemy fired a few cannon balls and shells during the day.

One incident I must relate. Gen[era]l Scott was sitting on his horse, a few rods in front of the line, about noon, the soldiers lazily reclining upon their arms, some preparing and some eating their dinner, when a shell was fired from the fort. In a moment we all saw it, and heard it buzzing through the air, and were all upon the look out to ascertain where it was going to fall. Gen[era]l Scott threw up his sword in such a manner as to take sight across it, at the bomb, and found that it would fall upon him and his charger, unless he made his escape instanter. He wheeled his spirited animal to the left, and buried his spurs in his sides. The whole army was gazing upon the scene with intense anxiety for the safety of their beloved commander, and with the highest admiration of his decision of Character in such an emergency, when the shell *actually dropped upon the very spot* he had a moment before occupied, and exploded without damage! I am not aware that this incident has ever been communicated to the public, at the time I am writing this.[57]

We now returned to Chippawa, without attacking the fort, which was deemed inexpedient, after lying before it for only a few hours, and ascertaining the amount of force within it, & the means of defense, in case of an attack.

On the 25th occurred the famous battle of "*Lundy's Lane*" or "*Bridgewater*", on a farm of "*Lundy*" nearly opposite Niagara Falls, about three miles below Chippawa.[58] It commenced at 7 o'clock P.M. and continued till 12 at night. The enemy had possessed himself of an eminence of ground in an open field, at his leisure, and planted his guns, formed his line, and made every other needful preparation to receive us.

Intelligence of these circumstances being given to Gen[era]l Brown, he ordered Gen[era]l Scott with his brigade to march forth and enter into an engagement, while he would make arrangements to re-inforce him with other troops, soon as it became necessary. This brigade consisted of the 9th, 11th, 22nd & 25th Infantry, with Towson's Artillery and a Squadron of horse. A solid column was formed, which marched to the field, under the influence of spirited martial music.[59]

When that part of the column in which I was situated had arrived within

---

[57] Here Hanks included a marginal notation: "December, 1842".

[58] The battle did not actually take place on William Lundy's farm but on and around a country road named for him.

[59] In actual fact, Brown had no knowledge of a British force being positioned along Lundy's Lane and sent Scott north from the camp on a reconnaissance in force. Scott encountered the British, and both armies poured in reinforcements during the battle that followed.

half a mile of the scene of action, We heard the firing commence, and saw some of the cavalry returning wounded, and heard the savage yell of the British Indians. I remember, a trumpeter was riding back, furiously, wounded, with the blood streaming, profusely down his temples & cheeks. As I was also a musician, I felt much alarmed for my own safety, not knowing but I should be in as bad or a worse situation in a few minutes. There was no stopping, nor escape, into battle we must go.

In coming in sight of the enemy we found his position as described above, and formed our line under his fire, both of Cannon and small arms. There was a small piece of wood, thro' which we passed to gain the open field where the battle was fought. A rail fence divided the field from the wood. Over this fence the soldiers were obliged to climb to obtain their places in the line. Many of them were shot and fell from the top of the fence, Killed and wounded. The cannon balls, grape shot,[60] & musket balls flew like hailstones, and yet we were not firing a gun. As soon as the men got their places in the line then they began to return the fire.

In these circumstances I met with what I consider the most narrow escape that I experienced while in the service. While sitting on the fence, for a single instant ready to jump off into the open lot, a charge of grape shot rattled around me with terrible threatening to my personal safety. They cut the branches of trees over my head, and on my right hand and on my left; also splintered the rails on either side and under my feet but not so much as the hair of my head was hurt! A thousand times have I reflected on this incident as the most wonderful Providential preservation from instant death; though I suppose I have been in as great danger, many times, but never so evident to myself as in this instance.

In this engagement Capt. Ketchum[61] passed around in the rear of the Enemy's line in the dark and took Gen[era]l Riall,[62] and several other British officers, prisoners, and returned safely with his company, which belonged to

---

[60] Grape shot was never utilized by British field artillery because it damaged the muzzles of the brass ordnance with which that service was equipped in 1814. What Hanks calls grape shot was, in reality, the bullets of either canister rounds or shrapnel shells.

[61] Captain Daniel Ketchum, 25th Infantry. This aptly named officer took numerous prisoners during the action.

[62] Major General Phineas Riall (1775-1850). A career soldier with very little combat experience, Riall commanded the Right Division of the British army in Canada and was responsible for the defense of the Niagara area in July 1814. He was defeated by Brown at Chippawa on July 5, 1814, and his capture at Lundy's Lane brought forward his superior, Lieutenant General Gordon Drummond, to command in the Niagara peninsula. Drummond proved a tougher opponent for the Americans.

"The most narrow escape that I experienced..."

the 25th Regt. Col[onel]. Miller,[63] too, signalized himself by taking twenty-five pieces of the enemy's cannon, at the point of the bayonet, and spiking them, and thus rendering them useless for the remainder of the contest.[64] There was also a Sergeant Thompson from the same town where I resided (Pawlet) who exhibited the most heroic bravery in a very dangerous position, and who was immediately promoted to the rank of an ensign, as a reward of merit.

Every regiment has a stand of colors consisting of two flags. The 11th to which I belonged, had one painted on blue and one on yellow silk. Sometimes they were both taken to the field, and sometimes only one. It is one of the first objects of contending armies to break the centres of regiments and lines and thus throw them into confusion. This is done as effectively as any other way by aiming at the colors, which are stationed in the centre of their respective regiments.

It is thought by many, that, as musicians are placed in the rear of the line, they are in consequence in less danger than the private soldiers who constitute the line. But, as the musicians are placed in the rear of the colors, in the centre of the regiment or battalion, and as the aim of enemies respectively is mainly to shoot down the flags, and as the falling or striking of a flag is a signal of surrender; it seems to me that musicians thus situated are in equal danger with any other portion of the army.[65]

During this engagement, nine different persons were shot down, under this flag, successively. At last, this Sergeant Festus Thompson took it and threw its folds to the breeze. He was wounded in the hip, and the staff was severed into splinters in his hand. But he again grasped it by the stump, and waved it triumphantly over his own, and his fellow soldiers" heads, until the close of the battle.

After many such incidents occurred; after hundreds on both sides had yielded up their life blood, as a sacrifice upon the altar of their country's honor; after multitudes had been disabled by their wounds, whose sighs and groans, and urgent entreaties for assistance, had been spent in vain upon the "desert air", but were smothered by the clangor of arms; this memorable battle closed,

---

[63] Colonel James Miller (1776-1851). A career soldier, Miller's modest reply to Brown's order to attack and take the British artillery during the action, "I'll try, sir," has become the stuff of legend. Miller continued in the army, rising to the rank of brigadier general. He was later customs collector of the port of Salem, Massachusetts.

[64] This is a gross exaggeration. There were no more than nine pieces of British artillery on the field, although Miller captured them all.

[65] Since the commanding officers of regiments took post near the colors so that they could easily be located in action, they also occupied positions of danger. At Lundy's Lane, seven of the ten American regimental commanders present were killed or wounded.

37

by apparent consent, and desire of both armies. They retreated from the scene at the same time, weary and exhausted. It has often been called a *"drawn game"*, as it was difficult to decide which inflicted or received the greatest amount of injury.[66]

6. *The Siege of Fort Erie, August to September, 1814*

The Americans soon returned to Fort Erie, and began to strengthen and add to the fortifications. The original fort consisted of two or three bastions and two stone buildings suitable for accommodating about one hundred men with their provisions and stores. We immediately commenced an embankment, of half a mile in length, terminating in a battery, which received the title of Towson's Battery.[67] Another embankment was also constructed, which connected the old fort with the river, running eastwardly, perhaps fifty or sixty rods. We were thus enclosed on all sides except the East, by a mud wall sufficiently strong to stop a cannon ball.

In a few days, the enemy followed us up the river, and planted himself about 300 yards North of the fort and began to intrench, and commenced a cannonade. Meanwhile, some of their men deserted from them and came to us, by whom we learned that Col[onel]. Drummond,[68] who had the command, had determined to attack us, on the night of the 15th of August. Preparations were immediately made for their reception, and every man was ordered, on that night, to sleep upon his arms.

The night was rainy, and extremely dark; & as anticipated, the attack commenced at two, in the morning. The enemy approached the two extreme points of our works, old Fort Erie, and Towson's Battery. By them, not a gun was fired. They came with bayonets, scaling ladders, hand Grenades and faggots. Every one of them was supplied with an extra half pint of rum for the strengthening, and whetting up his courage; to make him fierce and brave in the attack and reckless of danger to himself.

Towson's artillery vomited forth a sheet of flame for more than an hour, which repelled, successfully, the British from that point. Their main force, however, was directed against the old Fort. Into this, about two to three

---

[66] The casualties at Lundy's Lane were extremely heavy. The British army reported 878 killed, wounded and missing; the American army a total of 860 casualties. For a recent study of this bloody engagement, see Graves, *The Battle of Lundy's Lane.*

[67] Also called the Snake Hill battery.

[68] Hanks confuses Lieutenant General Gordon Drummond, who led the British besieging force, with Colonel William Drummond (no relation), who commanded the 104th Regiment of Foot.

hundreds of them succeeded in climbing by means of their ladders notwith-standing several of our cannon, and a plenty of musketry were employed in demolishing them. The voice of Col[onel]. Drummond was distinctly heard: *"Give the d____d Yankees no quarter!"* He was soon shot through the heart.[69]

In ten or fifteen minutes after they took possession of the bastion, and while they were bringing some of its guns to bear upon our 9th regiment, and raking them from one end to the other, as they lay along the short embankment, from the fort to the river, an awful explosion occurred, which blew up the bastion; sent, in a moment, near two hundred of our enemies into eternity; caused the remainder to retreat with terror, to their camp; and closed the contest, for the present.

It remains uncertain by what means the explosion took place. Many rumours were afloat, the next day, among the soldiers. We all were acquainted with the fact that there was a powder magazine under that bastion; but supposed it so secure that no accident could ignite it. Two of the most probable reports I shall record. 1st. In firing the cannon upon the 9th Regiment, our enemies pointed it down hill, which they were obliged to do, in order to do execution; for that regiment lay twenty or thirty feet below the level of the floor of the fort. In doing this, they actually forced the fire of the gun through the cracks in the floor, into the magazine beneath, & blew themselves up. 2nd. Fearing that the enemy would get into the fort, our officers previously caused a train to be laid from a distance to the magazine; and when the British had got in, in multitudes, fire was set to the train, which, in a moment caused the fatal result. It was also said that the soldier who performed this act, was, next day, offered his discharge from the army and a considerable sum of money, as a reward for his bravery.[70]

This explosion occurred just before daylight. During the forenoon, I inspected the awful scene. I counted 196 bodies lying in the ditch and about the fort; most of them dead; some dying. Their faces and hands were burned black, many of them were horribly mutilated. Here and there were legs, arms and heads, lying, in confusion, separated, by the concussion, from the trunks to which they had long been attached. One trunk I observed, deprived of all its limbs and head.[71]

---

[69] On the life of Colonel William Drummond, see Donald E. Graves, "William Drummond and the Battle of Fort Erie", *Canadian Military History,* I, Nos. 1 & 2 (1992), pp. 25-43.

[70] The cause of the explosion has never been clearly established. The probability is, as Hanks states, that the magazine was ignited by the blast from the gun the attackers had turned on the 9th Infantry.

[71] Only at New Orleans on January 8, 1815 did the British suffer more casualties in a single action during the war. The official report listed 905 dead, wounded and missing after the assault of August 15. In contrast, the Americans suffered 62 casualties.

Col[onel]. Drummond was laid under a cart. When I first saw him he was naked except his shirt. All the remainder of his clothing, his gold watch, sword, epaulettes, and money, had been plundered by some of our men. We even picked the pockets of those who were dead and dying in the ditch. In the course of the day, the soldier who got Drummond's watch, sold it to one of our officers, for a small sum compared with its real value.

A large hole was dug outside the fort, and these bodies thrown in and buried before night. The enemy was so devoid of humanity, that they fired on us, while we were engaged in this melancholy service.

The British now commenced a regular cannonade and bombardment, which continued with very little cessation until the 17th of September at which time our attack upon their works was made, which was called the "*Sortie of Fort Erie*". I shall relate a number of incidents to which I was personally witness, during those thirty-two days.

Men were stationed on the parapet constantly, to observe the motions of the enemy, whose works and guns were in full view. When a flash was seen, these sentinels were able to decide instantly whether it was a cannon, or a mortar; and that all might be in the best condition of safety, they would exclaim aloud "Shot" or "Shell", as the case might be. If a shot, every soldier hid himself in a moment behind the embankment, if he was not there already; if a shell, all eyes were turned upward, to ascertain where it was to fall, as described, in the case of Gen[era]l Scott, when we lay before Fort George.

The bomb shell is shot from a short gun, elevated in such a manner as that the track of the shell, passing to the point where it is to do execution, will form a curve line (a parabola), shorter or longer, according to the distance which it is to be propelled. The fuse is a plug of wood driven into the opening in the side of the shell, having a gimlet hole through it, which is filled with combustible matter, which ignites by the discharge of the mortar. The length and combustibility of the fuse, are proportioned to the distance likewise.

It is the common calculation to have the shell burst in the air just above the heads of its victims. Frequently, however, it falls into the ground and explodes, throwing its fragments with earth, gently and feebly around, without damage. Sometimes it does not burst at all, and after waiting a suitable time, a soldier digs it up, and finds the fuse smothered and put out by the earth coming into contact with it. In such cases, we used to put in a new fuse, and fire them back again, and occasionally enjoyed the barbarous satisfaction of seeing them fly to pieces in the immediate vicinity of their original proprietors. A similar use was made of several cannon balls which found a lodgement in our mud walls.

One day, several boats with militia from Buffalo, were landing on the shore near our camp in plain view of the enemy's batteries, when they were fired upon, and several men killed and one or two of the boats sunk. On another occasion, one of the cannon balls from the British came bounding along over the ground in a lazy manner, as though its force was nearly spent, when a soldier attempted to stop it as he would have done with one made of woollen yarn and covered with leather; but he soon found himself sadly mistaken in his estimate of its velocity and momentum when he saw it careering on its antic course for half or three quarters of a mile farther and losing itself in Lake Erie; leaving him minus a hand! He went to the hospital and submitted his arm to amputation.

Dan Ward was about eighteen years of age. His father was in the same company to which he and I belonged. They were also from the same town (Pawlet, or rather from the *edge of Wells*). The enemy frequently sent Shrapnel Shells at us. They are the size of a 32 lb. ball, and are shot by a 32 lb. long gun.[72] They are filled with powder, bullets, and fragments of rough and rusty iron, and are so managed as to explode just before they reach their victims, and throw their contents forwards and downwards. When they do execution according to their design, they are very destructive, often disabling several men at a single shot.

Two or three hundred men were sent out one afternoon to put *abbatis* into the ditch, outside of our works, the more effectually to defend us from any attack of the enemy's soldiery, that might thereafter be made. They performed the work in fifteen or twenty minutes but had a number of these shells fired among them during the time. Only one, however, did any harm. That wounded nine men. Dan Ward was one of them and he, with some others, died a day or two afterwards. He was wounded in the breast with a musket shot contained in the shell before it burst.

The word abbatis (pronounced ab-ba-tee) is French, but is adopted into the technical language of war. The thing itself is a tree of from four to six inches in diameter at the base, with all its limbs cut off, say three feet from the trunk leaving sharp points sticking out in various directions. Thousands of these put into the ditch, around the embankments, butts down, and points upwards and outward, would make it very difficult for assailants to pass through them until the assailed would have an opportunity of shooting them all down. It was impossible to pass by, or through them, as they were placed; while removing them, they could not use their arms; a decided advantage would be thus possessed by those within who by that means, would be morally certain to repel the invaders.

After the cannonade had continued for a few days, there seemed to be a tacit agreement between the parties to have a short cessation of firing at meal times and there was generally little activity during the night. At these times our

---

[72] In 1814 guns were denominated by the weight of round shot that they fired. Thus, a 32-pounder gun fired a solid shot weighing 32 pounds. Shrapnel shells were actually available for all the different calibers of British artillery.

soldiers would cook and eat their provisions, and expose themselves all over the camp ground as they would not dare to do, while the cannonade was progressing. Occasionally we were surprised by an unexpected shot before the usual time for the respite had expired when many were likely to be killed or wounded.

I remember a Corporal, by the name of White, who, one evening, was cooking some meat exposed to fire of the enemy, in the open Camp ground, when a hot shot was sent over. By heating, it had cracked into two parts, one of about one third, and one of about two thirds of its substance. The largest piece took off both of Corporal White's arms, above the elbows. They were immediately amputated and he got well. Of course he was discharged, and if living, must have a pension from the government, sufficient to support him and pay an attendant for feeding and otherwise assisting him.[73]

As there were no regular barbers attached to the army, the soldiers used to shave themselves, and each other. One morning several were shaving in succession, near a parapet. Sergeant [Wait] sat down facing the enemy, and Corporal [Reed] began to perform the operation of removing the beard from his face, when a cannon ball took of the Corporal's right hand, and the Sergeant's head; throwing blood, brains, hair, fragments of flesh and bones, upon a tent near them, and upon the clothing of several spectators of the horrible scene. The razor also disappeared and no vestige of it was ever seen afterwards. The Corporal went to the hospital and had his arm amputated, and a few men rolled up the Sergeant's body in his blanket, carried it out and buried it. Probably less than twenty minutes transpired, between the time he sat down to be shaved and the time he was reposing in the home of the soldier's grave![74]

I can never forget another man who was killed in an instant while apprehending little or no danger. He was a very large and tall soldier, upwards of six feet. He was reclining on his knapsack, supporting his head with his right hand and elbow, when a 10 1/2 inch shell exploded fifty or sixty feet above our heads. A large piece of it fell upon the center of his body, and cut him in two, as effectually and as instantaneously, as ever the axe of the guillotine severed the head [of] one of its victims. In a few moments, he too was wrapped up in his blanket, carried out and buried.

---

[73] In fact, this soldier, Private Robert White, was awarded a pension of $480 per year by the government. He married and had a family and was still living in 1860. See Benson J. Lossing, *Pictorial Field Book of the War of 1812* (New York, 1869), pp. 843-44n.

[74] The corporal's name was Reed, the sergeant was William Wait (or Waits). According to one source, "The day of his death, Wait was oppressed with a belief that some calamity awaited him, and was constantly asserting to his comrades that he should never live to visit home and the scenes of his childhood again." See Josiah Goodhue, *History of the Town of Shoreham, Vermont* (Middlebury, 1861), p. 103.

Several skirmishes took place between our picket guards, and squads of British soldiers at various times during August and the fore part of September. The enemy constructed a new battery farther west than those they were using from day to day; and, in order to bring it to bear upon us, they were obliged to cut down a number of large tress to make an opening. That they might do this without exciting our suspicion, and running the risk of having extensive slaughter by our cannon, they sent out a small scouting party to commence a fire upon our advance guards, hoping thus to engage the attention of all our force, with its officers. They succeeded in effecting their object by this means but not without the loss of lives on both sides.

One man near me was looking on, to witness this skirmish with multitudes of others not in action. We all supposed ourselves perfectly safe, as we stood behind our embankment with our heads and shoulders above it. A musket ball, however, reached this soldier, and hit him in the forehead. It split in two; half of it penetrating his brain and half falling at his feet. He lived only a day or two, before the wound proved fatal. The half bullet, very much put out of shape, was shown about among the soldiers for several weeks as evidence of that very remarkable occurrence.

Cannon balls would sometimes pass so near that we were almost knocked over by the pressure they produced upon the air. When this happened, and we were not hurt, we exclaimed *"that went as swift as any goose egg!"* This expression, I believe, was first uttered by one of the officers and reiterated a thousand times by the privates & musicians. It is singular that we could be so reckless in the midst of danger and death; but so it was.

There were perhaps a dozen houses in our enclosure, which were formerly occupied by citizens and composed a little village. These were now occupied by the officers, and as hospitals for the invalids. They were defended by mud parapets, on the side next the enemy and were considered comparatively safe from the effects of their long guns. Gen[era]l Gaines[75] had his quarters in one of these buildings. One day, he was lying on his bed, when a large shell descended through the roof, and two floors, into the cellar where it burst, filling the house with smoke, dirt and fragments of iron, wood, &c. The General was wounded slightly, which was all the harm that was done.

On the 17th of September, "the *sortie*" of Fort Erie was performed. "Sortie", I believe, means to attack an enemy who are besieging a fort or town. It was a rainy, dark day and probably they did not expect us to call on them just at that

---

[75] Brigadier General Edmund P. Gaines (1777-1849). Commissioned in the army in 1809, Gaines was a lieutenant colonel by the outbreak of the War of 1812. He was promoted to brigadier general in the spring of 1814 and assumed command of Fort Erie in early August. After Gaines was wounded, Brown resumed command of the Left Division.

"That went as swift as any goose egg..."

time. We passed through a deep ravine, which lay between them and us, and came within a few rods of them before they discovered our approach. A few men were left in the fort and the cannonading was continued with little abatement. When we came upon them, they seemed to be thunderstruck, and surrendered at pleasure. Their main army however, were two miles from that place in their tents. Without firing a musket we took thirteen Commissioned officers, 400 soldiers and spiked all their cannon, and cut to pieces their wheels, and blew up their powder magazine; after which we precipitately returned by the way we came. When I say we did not fire a musket, I mean not after we came up to the batteries. Previously, however, there was quite a little engagement, with their picket guards and several of our officers and men killed, among the former of whom was Capt. Hale[76] who commanded the company to which I was attached.[77]

7. *The End of the War*

In a very few days after this, the enemy withdrew, to Chippawa, and we soon evacuated the fort and crossed over to Black rock, and marched to Sackets Harbor, into winter quarters.[78] During the cold season, I was, much of my time, engaged in drawing plans of battles, fortifications, cantonments and harbors, on paper with water colors. The officers of my regiment, seeing some of them, encouraged me by purchasing what I had, and commissioning me to execute more, under their direction. The price they offered and paid me, was

---

[76] Captain Horace Hale, 11th Infantry.

[77] Because the British commander, Lieutenant General Gordon Drummond, had decided to lift the siege, the sortie of September 17, 1814 was a needless operation. Brown, of course, could not have known that. Casualties were heavy on both sides; the British reported a total of 516, the Americans 511. For a recent study of this engagement and the entire siege, see Whitehorne, *While Washington Burned.*

[78] Hanks is compressing time again. The Left Division, to which he belonged, remained in Canada until October 24, 1814 when it re-crossed the Niagara River and marched to Sackets Harbor.

[79] Considering that Hanks' pay was only eleven dollars per month, this extra money must have been agreeable. For the pay scale of the army in 1814, see *The Army Register of the United States* (Boston, 1814), pp. 106-09.

It is possible that at least one of Hanks' watercolors survives. Sackets Harbor State Historic Site has a small work entitled "Chase of the British Schooner Simcoe by the U.S. Sch[ooner]s Hamilton, Gov. Tompkins, and Julia". It depicts an incident of the 1813 naval campaign on Lake Ontario and might have been done by Hanks under the direction of a naval officer at Sackets Harbor. The watercolor is reproduced in Bowler, *War Along the Niagara,* p. 53 and back cover.

one dollar each.[79] Thus my talent for drawing and painting, was in a small degree, cultivated, under the most unfavorable ....[80]

.... In February, 1815, the news of peace reached us. As I had enlisted for "during the war", of course, my enlistment now expired. All the soldiers rejoiced, but none so heartily, as the "during the war's men". An extra gill[81] of whiskey was furnished to all, wherewith to make merry. I drank mine, so that I might feel good. Only once, before now, had I drank a gill at one draught, and that was for the purpose to trying my mettle. I drew a ration of whiskey (a gill) every day, but with these two exceptions, never drank it.

There was an old soldier by the name of Jemmy Thompson, who had liking for both me and my whiskey. He was naturally a kind and affectionate man, and enjoyed much pleasure in being benevolent. He took me under his charge soon after I entered the service, and always drank my ration of whiskey, for which he remunerated me, in washing my clothes, cooking my victuals with his, furnishing an extra blanket, and *hooking* anything we wanted, that he could get his hands on; besides exercising something like a general supervision over all my affairs.

I have often wondered why I did not consume my daily allowance of intoxicating liquor and become a drunkard. But I had no love for the "*fire water*", and never considered it a bad bargain that Jemmy Thompson disposed of it, at his pleasure. If I had habitually used it myself, I should have formed an uncontrollable appetite which would, long since, have laid me in the grave.

During my term of service, I was preserved from sickness, in a remarkable manner, having had only two weeks' illness within the twenty-six months I was in the army & that was so slight, that I was able to walk about the whole time. I endured many privations and hardships, at various times sleeping out in the open air in all kinds of weather, in rain, sleet and snow; in the woods and open fields; often weary and exhausted with marches for weeks together; sometimes being so hungry and having so little to satisfy the demands of *appetite,* as to be willing, eagerly to devour turnip peelings, floating in dirty water of a ferry boat; and on one occasion to eat what was decided to be "*horse beef*". On the night [of] the 2nd & 3rd of July 1814, when we crossed over from Black Rock to Fort Erie, I became so tired and sleepy that I slept, while marching, and standing still.

On the 23rd of May 1815 I was honorably discharged from the army, and return[ed] home in safety to my parents. When the acting Captain presented

---

[80] Unfortunately, the next two pages of the original manuscript were lost before the document was acquired by the Buffalo and Erie County Historical Society.

[81] A gill is a measure of four ounces.

me my discharge, he also accompanied it with the following papers, which had been prepared the same day without my knowledge; and I consider them the most flattering testimonials of the true estimation in which I was held by the Officers of the 11th Regt. The first is a letter from Lieutenant Isaac Clark, Jr.[82] who had commanded the company to which I belonged, ever since the death of Capt. Hale,[83] at Fort Erie, in September, 1814, and is as follows:

Sackets Harbor May 22 1815

Dear sir,

The bearer hereof, Jarvis F. Hanks, late a musician in my company, who has served during the war, with fidelity, and has since received an honorable discharge from me, is a worthy lad, and is [in] every way calculated for a military man, and one that would do honor to a military life. His parents reside in Pawlet and as I understand, are in rather low circumstances. I wish, Sir, you would use your influence to obtain a Cadet's warrant for him, in the army of the U. States. I shall obtain the recommendation of the officers of the regiment, and forward it to the war department. Hanks is about 15 years of age.

Isaac Clark, jr.,
Lt. 11th Infy.,
Commdn. Company

Col. Isaac Clark
26th Regt. Infy.

• • • • • • • • •

Sackets Harbor, May 23, 1815

Col. Isaac Clark,

In the discharge of an army it has been considered a general duty, to notice those who have made themselves conspicuous, by natural genius, acquired talents, or faithful services. Under this consideration, we the officers of the 11th Infantry, beg leave to recommend to your notice, *Jarvis F. Hanks*, son of Joseph Hanks, of Pawlet, as possessing

---

[82] First Lieutenant Isaac Clark, 11th Infantry. A native of Vermont, he was wounded at the sortie from Fort Erie, September 17, 1814.

[83] Captain Horace Hale, 11th Infantry. A native of Vermont, Hale was killed at the sortie from Fort Erie, September 17, 1814.

all the necessary qualifications for an useful military life.

We, therefore, earnestly request that you exert your influence to place him in the Military Academy, at West Point.

Jarvis Hanks is 15 years of age, and has *faithfully performed all the duties* of an excellent drummer and soldier, during the period of his enlistment.

Benja. Smead	Capt. 11th Infy.
M. Corning	Capt. 11th Infy.
H. Bedel	Lieut. 11th Infy.
Jac. Brown	Lieut. 11th Infy.
E. Bedford	Lieut. 11th Infy.
Alexr. S. Chadwick,	Lt. 11th Infy.
T. Dickey	Lieut. 11th Infy.
A. Rathbone	Ens. 11th Infy.

· · · · · · · · ·

When I arrived at home I proposed the subject of going to West Point to my father; but he was unwilling that I should be away from home any longer at present and consequently the above letters were never presented to Col[onel]. Clark, and I forever banished the desire to live a military life. On reviewing the circumstances and conclusions of that period, I am grateful, that I was left free to pursue the arts of peace, instead of the art of war, the former of which are more congenial to my disposition and happiness, notwithstanding the opinion entertained, and so favorably expressed in the letters above.

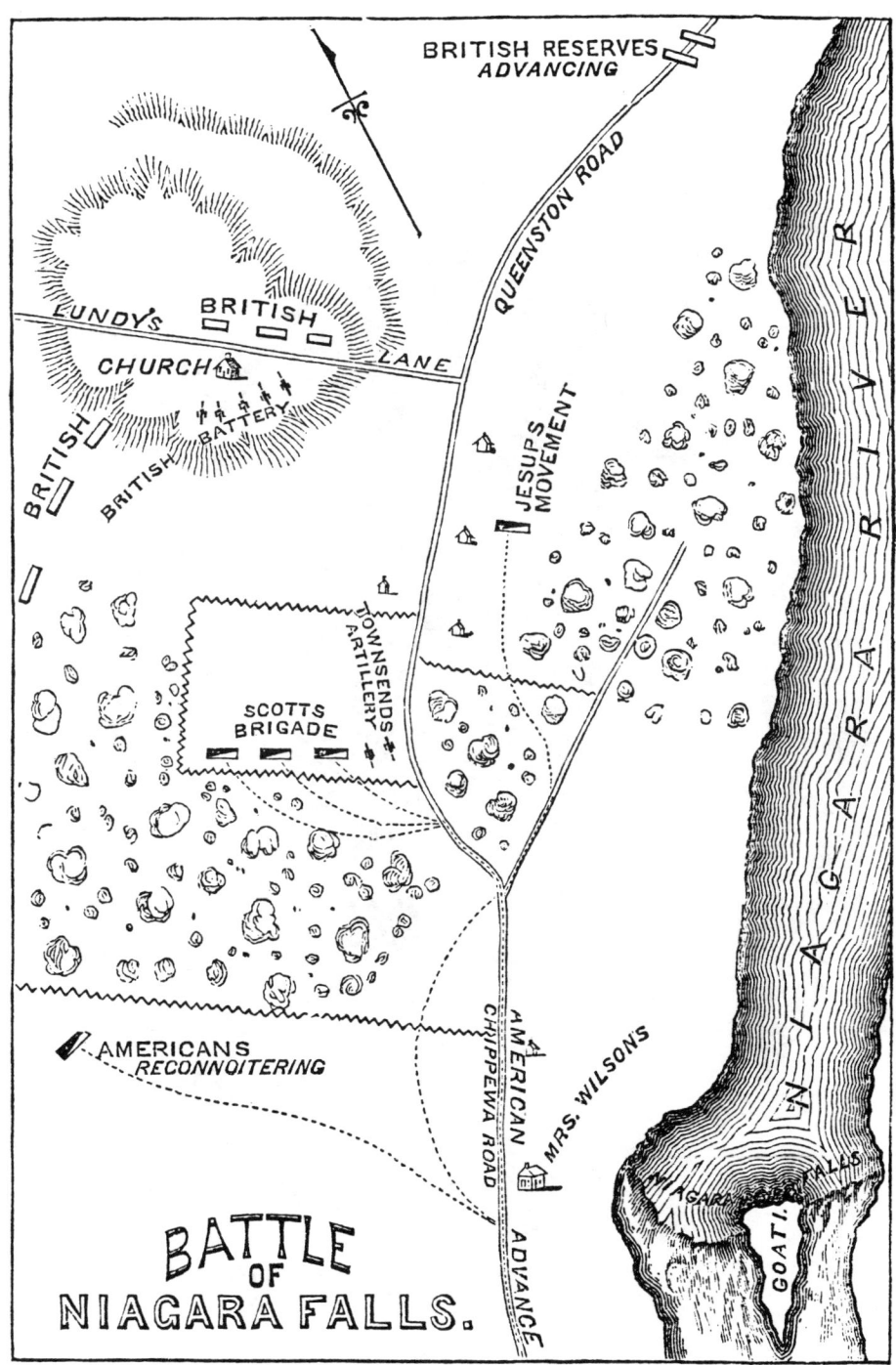

BRITISH RESERVES *ADVANCING*

QUEENSTON ROAD

LUNDY'S

BRITISH

CHURCH

LANE

BRITISH

BRITISH BATTERY

JESUPS MOVEMENT

TOWNSENDS ARTILLERY

SCOTTS BRIGADE

NIAGARA RIVER

AMERICANS *RECONNOITERING*

CHIPPEWA ROAD

AMERICAN ADVANCE

MRS. WILSONS

NIAGARA FALLS

GOAT I.

BATTLE
OF
NIAGARA FALLS.

A nineteenth century engraving from Benson J. Lossing's *Pictorial Field Book of the War of 1812* shows the preliminary maneuvers of the bloody battle of Lundy's Lane, fought on the evening of July 25, 1814.

Private ✐maſiah 𝓕ORD

23rd U.S. Infantry

II.

The Memoir of
Private Amasiah Ford,

23rd Infantry,

1813-1815

1. Campaign of 1813

I, Amasiah Ford, of the village of Ballston Spa,[84] in the County of Saratoga, State of New York, was forty-nine years old the 24th day of June 1845. In the year 1813, when I resided in the said village, I enlisted in the service of the United States February 18th, for during the war, under Lieutenant Azariah W. Odell in the 23rd Regiment of Infantry, commanded by Col. Brown.[85]

On the 14th April, marched to Greenbush — there mustered, then marched to Niagara, stopped at Fort Oswego a few days, then embarked on board batteaux and went up Lake Ontario to Fort Niagara. We arrived at Niagara in May and, on the 27th, embarked on board boats and landed on the Canada shore, under the command of Gen[era]l Dearborn[86] & took Fort George. On the 28th marched to Queenston & on the 29th back to Fort George. On the 5th June marched to Forty-Mile Creek & Stony Creek up the lake under the command of Generals Winder[87] & Chandler.[88]

On our arrival at that place we had a smart engagement with the enemy. On the 6th at night, it being very dark, we were attacked by the enemy with great

---

[84] A small village about six miles southwest of Saratoga Springs, New York.

[85] Colonel Daniel Brown, 23rd Infantry. Appointed commanding officer of that regiment in June 1812, Brown resigned in July 1813.

[86] Major General Henry Dearborn (1751-1829). A veteran of the Revolutionary War, Dearborn was appointed senior general of the army in 1812. He was relieved of his command on the northern frontier in the summer of 1813.

[87] Brigadier General William H. Winder (1775-1824). Winder never did have much luck. After being taken prisoner at the battle of Stony Creek, he was exchanged and appointed commanding officer of Military District No. 10 which included the city of Washington. He was defeated by the British again at the battle of Bladensburg in August 1814.

[88] Brigadier General John Chandler (1760-1841), from Massachusetts.

violence, but we soon beat them back & at day break on the 8th commenced our march back to Fort George; as we were out of provisions & had but very little ammunition to defend ourselves with.[89] We remained at Fort George all summer, having skirmishes with the enemy almost daily.

In the fall, General [James] Wilkinson sailed with his army up Lake Ontario & the river St. Lawrence from Fort George. The 23rd Regiment to which I belonged was left at the fort & in about a month 23rd Regiment had orders to march. The next day we crossed the river to the American shore under the command of Colonel Bissell[90] & left Major Chapin[91] with the brave volunteers in charge of Fort George. We had a forced march of about eighteen days in the cold season of the year through rain & mud (a great part of the way half up to our knees) & I lost my shoes from my feet in the mud marching through Cunarsharog hollow & travelled forty-five miles with my bare feet before I could get another pair to put on.

At the expiration of about eighteen days we arrived at Sackets Harbor. We remained at the Harbor in tents about one month (it being in the month of December) during which time we have heavy falls of snow. While at the Harbor we built us barracks & after they were finished we moved from our tents into them & enjoyed ourselves in them for three days when orders came to us to march & join Wilkinson's army at the French Mills. We marched the next day, December 25th.

Our march was through the Chateauguay woods about two hundred miles through great depths of snow, as the country through which we marched was all a wilderness. After a long and tedious march we arrived at the village of Malone about twelve miles from the French Mills. We stopped at this village one day when we marched to Chateauguay Four Corners, arriving there in the night. At this place we built barracks where we remained about five weeks & then marched to the French Mills & joined Wilkinson's army. We slept in the snow all night & the next morning the whole army took up its march for Plattsburgh.

---

[89] The battle of Stony Creek, fought June 6, 1813, was, tactically, a draw, but the decision of the American commander to retreat to Fort George after the action allowed the British to claim it as a victory. The action effectively marked the end of the 1813 American offensive on the Niagara.

[90] Colonel Daniel Bissell, 5th Infantry.

[91] Doctor Cyrenius Chapin was a prewar resident of Buffalo, New York, who raised a company of volunteers to assist the United States army in the Niagara. Many of their activities in the field were not military, and the unit was known to the regular officers as "Dr. Chapin and his Forty Thieves". The commander of American forces at Fort George in the autumn of 1813 was not Chapin, as Ford would have it, but Brigadier General George McClure of the New York Militia.

We remained at Plattsburgh until April 1814. In April the army under General Wilkinson marched into Lower Canada & attacked the enemy at the Stone Mill (LaColle Mill).[92] We had a smart engagement but soon retreated back to the village of Champlain then to Plattsburgh. I remained at that place until the 11th of June when the remaining part of the 23rd Regiment to which I belonged & a detachment of the 22nd were ordered to Buffalo under the command of Major Brooke[93] to join General Brown's army.

2. Lundy's Lane and the Niagara, July 1814

We arrived at Buffalo on the 3rd of July & marched to Lewiston on the 6th, crossed the river at that place on the 7th to Queenston in Upper Canada & joined General Brown's army. We remained at that place until the 11th when we attacked the enemy about four miles from Queenston at the village of St. Davids & drove them from the place besides taking their stores.[94]

We then marched within one mile of Fort George where we encamped two days & had some skirmishing with the enemy. At this time General Scott commanded the First Brigade & General Ripley the Second to which latter I belonged. We then took up our line of march back to Queenston heights & from thence to the village of Chippawa. We arrived at this place at night & at this time the enemy advanced on us with a heavy force. We crossed Chippawa Creek at that place & encamped on the 24th of July.

On the 25th the First Brigade commanded by General Scott marched down the river towards the falls & met the enemy at about 5 o'clock P.M. when the action commenced. Immediately the Second Brigade commanded by General Ripley, marched with quick step to the scene of action and soon advanced close to our enemy.

I belonged at this time to the first company commanded by Captain A.W. Odell, which was on piquet guard at the time. I was in the first platoon & when marching up in open column a party of the enemy which lay in ambush rose & fired upon us, when, out of thirty-two in the first platoon, only eight of us

---

[92] The battle of LaColle Mill in April 1814 marked the end of Major General James Wilkinson's long and colorful military career. He was soon after removed from command.

[93] Major George Brooke, 23rd Infantry (1785-1851). A native of Virginia, Brooke had a reputation as one of the bravest officers in the army. See John C. Fredriksen, *Officers of the War of 1812 with Portraits and Anecdotes* (Lewiston, NY, 1989), pp. 93-95.

[94] Actually, Colonel Isaac Stone's battalion of New York Volunteers ran wild at St. David's on July 11, 1814 and burned the little Canadian hamlet to the ground. For this act, General Brown dismissed Stone from the army the same day.

"Form, my good fellows..."

escaped the desperate slaughter. At this crisis the whole regiment broke up & scattered in every direction.

About this time Captain A.W. Odell arrived to take care of his company, which was commanded by his lieutenants & finding his company all broke up, what was left of them, exclaimed with a loud & desperate voice amidst the roar of cannon & musketry & the groans of the dying: "Is this my company in this situation? Form, my good fellows!" & at the exertions of the officers the Reg[imen]t. was soon brought into line of battle. Now the action commenced very desperate & severe.

At this time it got to be sometime in the evening & all the mark we had to fire at was the enemy's blaze. About this time the enemy made a desperate charge on us but we beat them back & followed up the charge at the point of the bayonet under the command of Colonel Miller & took the enemy's cannon which was placed upon an eminence nearly opposite the falls of Niagara.

The action lasted about three hours and forty minutes. Generals Brown and Scott both having been wounded & left the field, General Ripley now assumed the command. The troops at this time being fatigued & almost choked with thirst & it being late at night General Ripley thought proper to withdraw his men from the field of battle & retire to the village of Chippawa where his troops could take some refreshments & get some rest & accordingly they did.

The next morning we appeared before the eyes of the enemy as ready to engage again as ever. I that morning was one of about two hundred men who were detailed from the main army as a vanguard under the command of Lieutenant Tappan[95] to advance & commence the action anew with the enemy. When we advanced within musket shot of the enemy's line while they seemed to have no inclination to re-commence the engagement we soon had orders by express to return & join the main army, which we did. We then took up our line of march back to the village of Chippawa, burnt the town, crossed the bridge at that place, burnt that, & proceeded on our march to Fort Erie.

3. *The Siege of Fort Erie, August to September 1814*

We fortified this place against the enemy by building a breastwork & throwing out abbatis from the fort to the shores of Lake Erie. About this time the enemy advanced within one hundred rods of our garrison, built a battery on the bank of the Niagara & commenced a heavy cannonading upon us which

---

[95] First Lieutenant Samuel Tappan, 23rd Infantry. Throughout the Niagara campaign, Tappan served as a light infantry and reconnaissance specialist.

they continued for about four days & night.[96] In the meantime they built three more batteries[97] while they mounted on each of them four thirty-two pounders (iron pieces) for the same purposes.[98]

In the midst of the cannonading the enemy attacked us on the right & left flanks, the fort being on the right near the bank of the Niagara river & Towson's battery being on the left near the shore of Lake Erie. The enemy now made a desperate charge on these two points. Col. Drummond having command of the charge at the fort & exclaiming at almost every breath to his men: "Shew the damned Yankees no quarter!"

As soon as the action commenced the first & second companies of the 23rd Regiment were ordered to the fort & I, belonging to the first company, was amongst the rest. We immediately repaired to the fort which was about one hundred yards distant with double quick step. We took our post on the battlements in the front part of the fort where we kept our enemy off with our bayonets from scaling the walls until they forced us to retreat into the rear part of the fort when the magazine blew up & upwards of five hundred of the enemy were launched into eternity almost in an instant. Among the slain was Col. Drummond he was shot in the breast with a musket ball by some of the "damned Yankees" as he termed them. Day light now appeared & the enemy made their retreat back to their encampment. The American loss in this engagement was about seventeen, the British loss could not have been less than one thousand[99] for we took seventeen hundred stand of arms that morning.[100]

On the 17th of September our army under General Brown was once more formed in line at Fort Erie to sally out & storm the enemy's batteries which were erected a short distance from the fort for the purpose of cannonading on us as I have mentioned heretofore. We now took up our line of march for the scene of the action. The 23rd Regiment was ordered to attack battery & blockhouse No. 4 on the left & our Indians & Volunteers commanded by General Porter were on the extreme left of us. Perhaps it may be well to state here that those

---

[96] This is an exaggeration on Ford's part. The British bombardment commenced on August 13 and continued until dark on the 14th.

[97] In actual fact, only one battery had been completed by the time of the assault of August 15, 1814. Two more were constructed subsequently.

[98] This is also an exaggeration. Throughout the siege, the British were short of heavy artillery and did not possess this number of 32-pounder guns.

[99] The official British casualty return listed just under one thousand men killed, wounded captured, or missing during the night assault of August 15, 1814.

[100] A "stand of arms" consisted of a musket, its bayonet, cartridge box, and belt. Ford's figure would seem to be exaggerated.

fortifications were all in the skirts of the woods surrounding our encampment from the river to the shores of Lake Erie.

We now took up our line of march with firm & steady step to meet our enemy. We marched into the skirts of the woods & in a few minutes the enemy opened a brisk fire upon us. At this instant one of my messmates, Private Woolman,[101] was shot dead at my right side. Only imagine my feelings at this occurrence. They changed from a sense of fear to those of the bloodthirsty Wallace who exclaimed: "the blood of Marion cries for revenge & I will repay it!"[102]

We now charged upon the blockhouse from which the enemy kept up a brisk fire until they were compelled to surrender. Here we took about eighty prisoners while the ground was strewed with the dead bodies of the enemy. We now took our stations behind the enemy's breastworks while they retreated about eight rods further into the woods behind another breastwork. We kept up a brisk fire on the enemy for some time.

At this crisis, General Ripley was shot down by a ball striking him in the neck & was carried from the field but his wound did not prove mortal. About this time I was in the act of discharging my piece at a Red Coat [when] a ball passed through my cap directly under my cockade. I discharged my piece at my mark at the same time & never saw my mark again.

In this engagement we took three of the enemy's batteries, spiked their cannon, broke up the[ir] arms, cut down their carriages & dropped their pieces in the mud. We then returned to the fort.

The next morning (September 18th) the enemy had retreated from their works down the river.[103] Immediately, there was a detachment of about 150 men detailed from our army to reconnoiter their Rear Guard under the command of First Lieutenant Belknap.[104] I was one of the party; but unfortunately Lieutenant Belknap was shot through the thigh & we returned to the fort.

We remained at Fort Erie from about the 1st of August to the 1st of October encountering heavy cannonading while the balls & bombshells & grapeshot

---

[101] No soldier of this name appears on the official casualty records of the 23rd Infantry at the siege of Fort Erie.

[102] The source of this quotation is obscure.

[103] This is an error. The British army retreated from Fort Erie on September 21, 1814 and had been planning to withdraw when Brown's troops sortied on the 17th of that month.

[104] Second Lieutenant William Belknap, 23rd Infantry (1794-1851). Belknap played a prominent role during the siege of Fort Erie and later rose to command a brigade during the Mexican War.

were flying & bursting among us almost without cessation and to cap the climax some of us were skirmishing with the enemy almost daily.

4. The End of the War

About this time General Izard[105] who had been all summer with about twelve thousand men marching from Plattsburgh crossed the river to reinforce General Brown who was fighting in an enemy's country all summer almost daily, with only a small handful of men. Gen. Izard crossed with army to Black Creek. After Izard crossed into Canada with his army, General Brown crossed to the American shore. Our army now left Fort Erie & joined Izard's at Black Creek.[106] We then took our line of march under General Izard for Chippawa. When within about a mile of that place we were attacked by the enemy and passed some shots. Here we encamped on the banks of the Niagara river, when a detachment of about fifteen hundred men were ordered up Chippawa Creek, about ten miles to reconnoiter the enemy at that place.

The next day on the arrival of the Americans they met the enemy and had a smart engagement with a superior number of men for about two hours. Then the Second Brigade to which I belonged was ordered to the scene of action as a reinforcement. Accordingly we were soon on the march.[107]

We had not been long on the way before the rain began to fall very fast. We continued our march through a most dismal swamp in the mud up to our knees & at length arrived about sunset on the opposite shore in a cleared field without anything to eat or cover our wearied bodies with as we had left our knapsacks behind and brought nothing with us but our muskets & cartridge boxes well filled with powder & ball.

Here we encamped for the night & built up large fires of rails, &c. to warm ourselves by, as it was now October & the weather very cold. Our stomach now

---

[105] Major General George Izard (1776-1828). One of the few general officers in the regular army to have been blessed with a formal European military education, Izard commanded the Right Division in the summer of 1814. Contrary to Ford's mistaken belief, it did not take him all summer to march to the Niagara — he did not leave Plattsburgh until early August and was delayed at Sackets Harbor. Izard's march, nonetheless, earned him the soldiers' nickname of "Amberzard".

[106] The original manuscript states "Black Rock" instead of "Black Creek". As the former is in the United States and the latter is in Canada, it is obvious from the context in which the term is used that Ford means Black Creek.

[107] A reference to the battle of Cook's Mills or Lyon's Creek, the last major engagement of the Niagara campaign. It was fought on October 19, 1814 between troops of Izard's Right Division and the British.

began to crave for food for we had not anything to eat; but, at length our officers procured a beef. We killed it & every officer & soldier helped himself to what he needed & roasted it in the fire by means of a sharpened stick & ate it without any salt to season or bread to eat it with.

Our appetites being satisfied, my comrades laid themselves down around the fires on the cold wet ground to rest their wearied limbs. I slept that night with my Captain (A.W. Odell) on some rails that we put down for that purpose to keep our bodies from the damp ground.

The next morning we took our breakfast as usual on fresh beef without salt but we found a substitute for bread by roasting pumpkins in the fire & eating them with our beef. We lived in this situation for two days & nights lying on the cold wet ground without anything to cover us but the bare curtain of Heaven, while the rain was pouring down in torrents upon us. When we returned to our encampment, the Army was on the march to Black Creek & we were obliged to march eight or nine miles further before we could draw rations. We arrived at Black Creek in the dusk of the evening, pitched our tents, built fires & drew rations and I must say that this was the best meal I ever ate for it consisted of raw pork & bread.

We stopped at this place three days & then General Brown's army crossed the river to the American shore, marched to Buffalo & from thence to Eleven-Mile Creek. Here we encamped a few days & then took up our line of march for Sackets Harbor. We arrived at the Harbor after a cold & tedious march where we took up our winter quarters. Here, we remained all winter in our barracks.

In February [1815] we heard of the great defeat of our enemy which was obtained over that hostile foe by General Jackson[108] & his brave troops at the battle of New Orleans when orders were given by our commanding officer to fire a salute when the Cannons in the garrisons & on board the fleet echoed the name of the Hero of New Orleans.

In March the joyful news of Peace rung in our ears & on the 24th of March 1815 the National Salute was fired & at night the village, barracks & fleet were illuminated.

I remained at Sackets Harbor until the 5th day of June 1815, having been in the service of my country two years, four months, eighteen days when I was honorably discharged from the Army of the United States and returned to my native village.

Amasiah Ford

---

[108] Major General Andrew Jackson (1767-1845) who gained a signal victory over a British force at New Orleans on January 8, 1815.

Private **Alexander MᶜMULLEN**

Fenton's Pennsylvania Regiment

III.

The Narrative of Alexander McMullen, a Private Soldier

in Colonel Fenton's

Regiment of Pennsylvania Volunteers

1. Call to Service and the March to Erie

During the late war, on or about the 20th of February, 1814, a draft of one thousand men was ordered by Simon Snyder, then Governor of the State, from the counties of Franklin, Cumberland, York, and Adams. Cumberland was to furnish one-half of this quota, and the remaining five hundred was divided among the other counties. Colonel James Fenton[109] was appointed to command the detachment, and Robert Bull,[110] Lieutenant-Colonel.[111]

My brother, James, being of the first class[112] in a company of militia, was drafted for six months. He was twenty-one years of age and of a delicate constitution. It was thought by a council of the family and friends that it would not do for him to go. My father was at that time an advocate and partisan for the measures of Government, and he then saw the evils of war.[113] I was about

---

[109] Colonel James B. Fenton from Newville, Cumberland County, Pennsylvania.

[110] Lieutenant Colonel Robert Bull, killed at Chippawa, July 5, 1814.

[111] Fenton's Regiment, officially known as the 5th Pennsylvania Volunteer Regiment, originated from a request by the federal government to Pennsylvania Governor Simon Snyder for volunteers to guard the Lake Erie borders of the United States. The unit was composed of elements of the 1st and 2nd Brigades of the 7th Militia Division of Pennsylvania and the 2nd Brigade of the 5th Division, both drafted men and volunteers. It was mustered into service at Carlisle in early March 1814 and mustered out of service at Buffalo on August 26, 1814. See Whitehorne, *While Washington Burned*, Annex G.

[112] "Being of the first class" — that is, the author's brother, a young, single male, was of the classification of state militia liable to be drafted for service. Older and married men belonged to classes less likely to be called out for extended service.

[113] McMullen's father was a staunch supporter of the war policies of President Madison's government. After one of his sons was drafted for military service, however, he apparently changed his tune.

two years older and more robust than my brother and offered myself, to which my parents, with some reluctance, consented.

The quota from Franklin rendezvoused at Loudon on the 1st of March, 1814. There was two companies of drafts, under command of Captain Samuel Gordon[114] and Jacob Stake,[115] and our company of volunteers under Captain Samuel Dunn.[116] These were all under command of Major James Wood.[117] W[illiam]m. McClelland, Brigade Inspector, was to furnish the tents and rations for these companies but for some reason they were detained, and we remained there for three days amid a continual scene of dissipation.

The tents arriving, we commenced our march for Lake Erie on Monday, the 4th [of March 1814], and crossed the North Mountain to McConnelsburg, in Bedford County, where the tents were pitched, straw provided, and we began to assume a military appearance. On Sidling Hill we first heard of the Cumberland volunteers. They had come by the Fannetsburg road. We were a short distance before them at the junction of the roads, an advantage which our officers wisely determined to keep, as by this we were much better supplied with the necessary articles on the road. On the 16th [of March] we arrived at Pittsburgh, and, crossing the Allegheny River, encamped on the plains in view of that city. The Cumberland men, coming the next day, encamped on Grant's Hill.[118] Here we received six dollars for three months' pay in advance from the State. The Legislature had granted this in addition to the United States' pay, making altogether ten dollars a month.[119]

After a stay of three days we commenced our march for Erie, then a small town, where we arrived after travelling through a deep snow and swampy roads for ten days, with no better beds than hemlock branches and an Indian blanket for a cover. We arrived in tolerable health and fine spirits on the evening of the last day of March, and encamped on a hill east of the village in view of Lake

---

114 Captain Samuel Gordon from Waynesboro, Franklin County, Pennsylvania.

115 This officer does not appear in official records.

116 Captain Samuel Dunn from Mercersburg, Franklin County.

117 Major James Wood from Greencastle, Franklin County.

118 The route taken by the Pennsylvanians on the march from Carlisle to Pittsburgh along the famous "Forbes Road" was essentially that used by the British in 1758 when they captured the Forks of the Ohio from the French. Grant's Hill was the scene of the defeat of a detachment of Forbes' army by the French in September of that year. See Fredriksen, "The Pennsylvania Volunteers in the War of 1812", p. 127.

119 The generosity of the state legislature meant that these militia privates were better paid than private soldiers of the regular army who received only eight dollars per month.

Erie. An old blockhouse stood between us and the lake, and a new one, nearly finished, beside it, with four pieces of brass cannon belonging to the State, making us safe from the enemy on that side. The Cumberland volunteers and the drafts from York and Adams arrived, and the regiment was organized into ten companies of one hundred men each. In a few days dissatisfaction began to appear in several companies, owing to the quality of the provisions. The flour was mouldy and the beef and pork unfit to be eaten. Desertions began to be frequent, but the offenders, being followed and brought back, were placed in the guardhouse, and generally punished by being marched in front of the regiment to the tune of the "Rogue's March."[120]

About the 20th [of March], Major Marlin[121] with a battalion of regulars took his station at the blockhouses. He was an officer of prepossessing appearance but of intemperate habits. About this time he made a call on Fenton's regiment for volunteers to go with him to Put-in-Bay to bring the scattered vessels of Perry's fleet[122] and a battalion of regulars commanded by Colonel Campbell.[123] He was furnished with about three hundred men, and set sail for Put-in-Bay in the fleet that had been anchored at Erie during the winter preceding. In about ten days they returned in consequence of bad weather. Our men, who had not been accustomed to nautical life, were glad to get their feet on solid ground once more.

2. The Raid on Long Point, Upper Canada

Campbell now took command of the regulars, who were considerably reinforced, and in the course of a few days planned an expedition to Long Point in Canada. He wanted as many volunteers from Fenton's regiment as he could get. Fenton agreed to go himself, and more than one-half of his men. We embarked in the fleet in the evening, and set sail at dark.[124] The weather was

---

[120] The use of this famous old tune as a symbol of military shame seems to have been widespread throughout United States forces, both regular and militia, during the War of 1812. See the reference in the memoir of Jarvis Hanks (note 36).

[121] Major Ralph Marlin, 22nd Infantry.

[122] This was the fleet constructed on Lake Erie in 1813 by Commander Oliver Hazard Perry. Following Perry's triumph over the British fleet in September 1813, the fleet anchored at Put-in-Bay for the winter.

[123] Lieutenant Colonel John B. Campbell, 19th Infantry.

[124] The expedition sailed on the evening of May 13, 1814.

"Some of us who were farmers had a curiosity..."

hazy, with very little wind, and next morning we were still in sight and not very far from the American shore. About eight o'clock the wind favored us, and towards sunset we cast anchor at Long Point. The landing of the troops now commenced. A party of British light horsemen waited on the bank till the men came within a short distance of the shore, then fired a volley and galloped off. We remained on the shore of the lake during the night without any disturbance.

The next morning [we] crossed a creek which emptied into the lake at this place, and had not proceeded far before [we] were fired upon by a party of Canadians. The fire was returned, and we took up the line of march for Dover, a small village about three miles from the lake. The situation of this village was pleasant, the houses generally frame, near a beautiful creek with a fine large fulling-mill, grist-mill, and saw-mill. The inhabitants had principally left town on our approach. We were then placed in line of battle, the artillery in the centre, the regulars on the right, a reserve in the rear, and a company, I suppose of observation, some distance off. An order from Campbell to set fire to the houses was now executed by men detailed from all the companies. A scene of destruction and plunder now ensued, which beggars all description. In a short time the houses, mills, and barns were all consumed, and a beautiful village, which the sun shone on in splendor that morning, was before two o'clock a heap of smoking ruins. The women and children had remained in the village and were permitted to carry out the valuable part of their moveable property. A party of sailors appointed to man the artillery killed the hogs in the streets, and severing them in the middle carried of the hind parts, while the head and shoulders were left in the street.

The line of march was now taken up the lake. The army halted about a mile from the lake at the house of a respectable looking German and as it had been ascertained that the British had no force of any consequence in that neighbourhood the men were permitted to stroll from the ranks. A short distance from this house was a pasture lot, in which grazed a fine English cow. Some of us who were farmers had a curiosity to examine this fine animal more closely. This drew a small group together, when a private of Gordon's company fired his musket and broke both her fore legs. The farmer and his family said nothing, afraid, I suppose, that their own turn might come next, and the officers, taken up in examining some Canadian prisoners, paid but little attention to it.

The sun was setting as the troops re-embarked, and shortly after dark we set sail, expecting to wake in the harbor of Erie, but judge of our surprise in the morning to find that we were not more than a mile from the Canadian shore and four miles from where we started the evening before. The sails were lowered, the fleet stopped and boats manned for shore. A troop of horse, formed on the shore, seemed determined to oppose our landing, but the turning of a long 32-pounder [gun] on board the *Porcupine* gun-boat[125] to bear on them, made them gallop off without firing a gun. There was a grist-mill and saw-mill, to which our forces set fire. Orders were then given to re-embark, and the fleet set sail for Erie, where we arrived next evening at dark, generally disgusted with the conduct of Campbell.[126]

3. An Act of Mutiny and the Camp at Buffalo

When we came back to the camp, we found that a number of men belonging to several companies had deserted, taking advantage of the absence of the officers. A short time after this a mutiny was set on foot by some designing men, who made the soldiers believe that the field officers and contractors were swindling them by buying up bad provisions at a low price, and that good could be bought if the officers wanted it. Another reason was that they had now been in the service nearly three months and had received but the six dollars from the State, and as we expected in a few days to march to Buffalo and be under the United States' officers, they were told that unless they stood out for their rights then, there would be no use of doing it at Buffalo.

A paper was drawn up and signed by a number, who were resolved not to start without two months' pay. The officers for some reason appeared but little concerned about it. The morning came to start for Buffalo. Preparations were made by those who were not in the conspiracy to start, and leave the mutineers if they were too strong to be forced off. The mutineers had loaded their muskets and had supplied themselves with cartridges, apparently determined not to

---

125 USS *Porcupine*, a gunboat/schooner, carried one 32-pounder gun and two 12-pounders. Launched in the spring of 1813, she was at the battle of Lake Erie in September of that year. *Porcupine* was very nearly captured along with two other American schooners, *Somers* and *Ohio*, during a British "cutting-out" expedition on August 12, 1814. She was sold out of the navy in 1825 and was for many years employed as a freight carrier on Lake Erie before being beached near Grand Haven, Michigan, in 1873. See James L. Mooney (ed.), *Dictionary of American Naval Fighting Ships*, Vol. VI (Washington, 1969), pp. 352-53.

126 Following his arrival at Buffalo, Campbell was suspended from duty, on the orders of the Secretary of War, pending an investigation into his activities at Long Point. A court of inquiry headed by Brigadier General Winfield Scott found that he had erred in destroying private property but returned him to duty.

The widespread devastation at Long Point so exasperated Lieutenant General Sir George Prevost, the British commander-in-chief, that he appealed to his naval counterpart, Vice Admiral Alexander Cochrane, to retaliate in kind on the Atlantic coast of the United States. Cochrane did so, and the result was a destructive British campaign in Chesapeake Bay culminating in the capture and burning of Washington in mid-August 1814. See Graves, *The Battle of Lundy's Lane*, chapters 2 and 13.

strike a tent without money. The regiment had been formed, roll called, and wagons all ready to load. Orders were given to strike the tents. About half were struck. The remainder stood, the owners beside them with loaded muskets. Colonel Fenton began to remonstrate, but they treated all he said with indifference.

The Adjutant, Thomas Poe,[127] standing beside him, indignant at such conduct, wanted the Colonel to use force, but he declined, and at Poe's request, gave him leave to quell the disturbance. The first company, a finely uniformed company of infantry from Carlisle, had been active in the mutiny, but their tents fell before the drawn sword of the Adjutant, and men who appeared determined to die on the spot, now shrank like children before one man. The rest followed their example, and in less than an hour the leaders of the mutiny were placed in the blockhouse in irons and the regiment was on its way to Buffalo.[128]

This march was a very pleasant one; vegetation was coming on with great vigour, and the country was fast being settled by respectable and intelligent looking men from the eastern States. After a march of eight days[129] we arrived on the banks of the Buffalo Creek, where we were met by a fine looking band of musicians, who escorted us to the village. This village had been burnt the winter before by the British and Indians. The inhabitants were generally living in sheds of frame lined with rough boards, a temporary protection from the inclemency of the weather. West of the town and between it and the lake was the encampment of the grand army said to be 2,500 strong. These were commanded by Major-General Jacob Brown. A regiment of artillery was on the northeast. We encamped on the left of the regulars in a piece of bushy ground, which was soon cleared off, making it a beautiful spot, with a fine spring close by the encampment.

Regulations new to us and very strict were now adopted. We rose at 4 o'clock (reveille beat) and answered to our names. We had fifteen minutes to prepare for drill, which generally lasted one hour. Breakfast being over, the regiment was formed, roll again called, guards detailed, and the regiment dismissed for a short time. The Sergeants' drill came next, which generally lasted till eleven

---

[127] Lieutenant Thomas Poe, adjutant of Fenton's Regiment. He died of wounds on July 26, 1814.

[128] Captain Samuel White has left a lengthy account of this near-mutiny. See his *History of the American Troops during the Late War, under the Command of Colonels Fenton and Campbell* (Baltimore, 1830), pp. 9-11.

[129] According to the anonymous diary of a volunteer from Cumberland County, Fenton's Pennsylvanians arrived at Buffalo on June 12, 1814. See Fredriksen, "The Pennsylvania Volunteers in the War of 1812", p. 148. A portion of the regiment sailed to Buffalo from Erie. See Joseph E. Walker (ed.), "A Soldier's Diary for 1814", *Pennsylvania History*, XII (1945), p. 298.

o'clock. At two the Adjutant-General[130] drilled, which was then dismissed till nine, when the roll was again called and we retired to rest. The time passed away in this manner, constant exercise, wholesome provisions, and strict discipline soon made our regiment have another appearance.[131]

4. The Battle of Chippawa

On the evening of the third day of July the regulars left their camp and marched down to the Niagara River, crossed during the night and surrounded Fort Erie, which surrendered the next day. There was but one battalion in the fort and two companies of artillery.[132] These were brought to Buffalo and from thence sent to Greenbush in the State of New York, escorted by Captain Alexander's[133] company of infantry. We crossed on the 5th. Some out of each company refused to go, and some of their comrades were detailed to bring them by force, which we found to be no easy matter, as they had taken possession of an old battery and stood in their own defence.[134] They were about eighty strong. A treaty was now commenced, and about twenty of them with their leader agreed to come over. The rest we left, our commander wisely considering them of little consequence.

The next morning we marched for Chippawa. The regulars had started the day before. About two o'clock we halted about two miles from the creek, where a large body of Indians of different tribes were preparing to go out on a scouting expedition. One of their chiefs in a speech, which for gesture and strength of lungs I had never heard equalled, was preparing them for bloody battle.

---

[130] Colonel Charles Kitchell Gardner (1786-1866), adjutant general of Brown's Left Division.

[131] The discipline in Scott's camp at Buffalo impressed the Pennsylvania citizen-soldiers. The anonymous volunteer from Cumberland County recorded that: "We live well here, but eat no idle bread, for drilling and parading occupies our attention nearly from revelee [sic] to 10 A.M. and in the afternoon we drill in regiment instructed by the Adjutant General Gardner whose presence among us commands immediate attention and respect, and while under him we consider ourselves as having a commander, a friend and instructor." Fredriksen, "The Pennsylvania Volunteers in the War of 1812", p. 150.

[132] This is an exaggeration. The garrison of Fort Erie consisted of a company of the 100th Regiment of Foot and detachments of the 19th Light Dragoons and Royal Regiment of Artillery, a total of 10 officers and 155 men. See Abstract of Weekly Distribution Return of the Right Division, June 22, 1814 in Cruikshank, *Documentary History*, I, pp. 28-30.

[133] Captain William Alexander from Carlisle, Cumberland County, Pennsylvania.

[134] What McMullen is saying is that some of the Pennsylvanians stood on their constitutional rights that they were not required to serve outside the boundaries of the territorial United States.

Volunteers were now called for from Porter's brigade. The Indians had started towards a pine wood back of the fields, where we halted. Having lost my sleep the night before — I had, like a simpleton, lent my musket to Lieut. Dick[135] — and lying down in a fence corner, fell fast asleep. In a few minutes the sharp crack of the Indians' rifles waked me. The noise was increased by the quick discharge of cannon and musketry. I ran to Major Wood, who was forming the regiment, and asked him what they were doing. "Fighting!" was the answer, "Fall into the ranks."

I now felt my situation, without gun or cartridge box. I ran to the bank of the river, where a boat was lying which had brought the baggage down the river, and solicited a gun, which after some difficulty I obtained, and soon joined our company. Just at this time I saw the Indians and some of the volunteers flying across the fields towards us. They had received a warmer reception than they expected.

Shortly after they crossed into the woods they came on a party of Canadian Indians and militia, who fired on them. The fire was returned and the Canadians fled towards the bridge, our volunteers in full pursuit. A number of the Canadian Indians and their militia lost their lives in this running fight. Approaching the bridges, they met the British army. A retreat now commenced, with the Canadians and some British regulars in full pursuit. In this retreat Robt. McClelland, a very respectable man of our company, lost his life. Almost all of the companies of our regiment lost some men.[136]

By the time the regiment came in view of Chippawa Creek the battle was over and the British retreating across the bridge. A number of killed and wounded lay on the plains where the army had fought. We marched past them towards the bridge, saluted by the cannon balls from the British works at Chippawa, which to us militia was a new but not a very pleasant sight. After keeping us a considerable time in front and exposed to the cannon of the British works, we were marched back to our camp. That evening we were joined by a company of Canadian volunteers who had entered the service of the United States.[137]

---

[135] First Lieutenant William Dick from Mercersburg, Franklin County, Pennsylvania.

[136] The official casualty return for Fenton's Regiment at Chippawa was 3 killed, 2 wounded and 7 missing. See Report of the killed and wounded of the Left Division, July 5, 1814, in Cruikshank, *Documentary History,* I, p. 43.

[137] The Canadian Volunteers were a small unit of Canadian renegades commanded by Joseph Willcocks, a former newspaper editor and member of the Legislative Assembly of Upper Canada. Commissioned as a lieutenant colonel in the United States service, Willcocks raised his corps of Volunteers who rendered good service as scouts to the American army in the campaigns of 1813 and

...(continued next page)...

The next morning the dead of both armies were buried. The killed and wounded amounted to six or seven hundred, of which the greater part belonged to the British.[138] Colonel Robert Bull,[139] second in command, Major Galloway[140] and Captain White,[141] were taken prisoners, besides a number of privates.

About twelve o'clock a number of men of different companies were detailed to take the prisoners who were all wounded, up the Niagara in boats to Buffalo. I was one of this party. The navigation of this stream up the river is very difficult and laborious. It was dark by the time we got eight miles, and as we were very tired we landed opposite a house on the shore to rest till morning. The owner had left this when the army came down the river.

As some of the men were slightly hurt and we in an enemy's country, a sentinel was set to watch the boat. About midnight my turn came. The moon gave but little light, and the prisoners and our men were all laying quiet, when the sound of footsteps within a few paces startled me. I turned hastily around and saw a large Indian, who when he saw my musket presented called out, "Don't shoot!" He proved to be one from our own side on his road to join the army.

The next day [7 July 1814] we arrived at Buffalo, where we were detained for eight days, when we returned to join the army, who were encamped at Queenston below the Falls of Niagara. The river at this town is narrow and very deep. Above the town was a steep hill, called Queenston Mountain, on the top of which was a fort where the volunteers and Indians were encamped. The New York volunteers having joined us, we were formed into a brigade, commanded by General Peter B. Porter.[142] After a march to the neighbourhood of Fort

---

1814. They committed many depredations on their former neighbors and citizens. For a history of the unit, see Donald E. Graves, "Joseph Willcocks and the Canadian Volunteers: An Account of Political Disaffection in Upper Canada during the War of 1812", M.A. Thesis, Carleton University, Ottawa, 1982. A complete muster roll for the Volunteers may be found in Whitehorne, *While Washington Burned,* Annex H.

[138] McMullen exaggerates here. The official casualty returns list 58 Americans and 148 British killed.

[139] Actually, Bull was killed by British Indians after he was taken prisoner. See White, *History of the American Troops,* pp. 18-19.

[140] Major Samuel Galloway.

[141] Captain Samuel White from Gettysburg, Adams County, Pennsylvania. White's own account of this action is found on pages 14-21 of his *History of the American Troops.*

[142] Brigadier General Peter B. Porter (1773-1844) of the New York Militia. A former member of Congress and a New York militia officer who resided in Black Rock near Buffalo. Porter was

George, where we remained two days, we returned to our former camp at Queenston.

On our march up the river, when we came in view of Queenston Heights, we discovered a number of the Canadian militia, who had taken possession of our former encampment. On our approach they began to move off. We pursued them for some miles. Being on a flanking party with others our route was principally through the woods. We returned in the evening with eight prisoners, most of them officers.[143]

5. *The Battle of Lundy's Lane*

Next day [24 July 1814] we marched to Chippawa and encamped. There was preparation making to march to Burlington Heights, but on the evening of the 25th July intelligence was brought that the enemy were in pursuit of use and coming up the river below the Falls. General Scott, with his brigade went to meet them, and gave them battle about three miles from the camp. The second brigade of regulars, under General Ripley, hastened to his support, and the contest became warm and bloody.

The enemy's artillery being taken about the time we of Porter's brigade arrived on the battle ground, the enemy reinforced and came down the hill directly in front of us. The brigade[144] was just formed into line, and I heard the voice of Porter saying to us, "Show yourselves men, and assist your brethren!" when showers of musket balls came over our heads like a sweeping hail storm. We returned the fire from the whole line of the brigade. The firing was now kept up from both sides with great spirit, but it was soon evident that there was a great advantage on our side. The ground the British occupied was consider-

---

appointed to command the 3rd Brigade of Brown's Left Division which consisted of Fenton's Pennsylvania regiment, Willcocks' Canadian Volunteers and a strong force of New York militia commanded by New York Brigadier General John Swift comprising Colonel Philetus Swift's regiment of New York militia volunteers, Lieutenant Colonel Isaac W. Stone's battalion, New York militia detached, Captain Hope Davis' light infantry company, and Captain Claudius V. Boughton's mounted company. Completing Porter's brigade was a large force or 400 to 500 native warriors from the Seneca, Tuscarora, Onondaga, Delaware, and Oneida nations.

143 Captain William H. Merritt of the Canadian militia has left an account of this action from the opposing side. See William H. Merritt, *Journal of Events, Principally on the Detroit and Niagara Frontiers during the War of 1812* (St. Catharines, Ont., 1863), pp. 59-61.

144 It should be noted that, because of detachments made from his command to garrison Lewiston and to guard both prisoners and the camp at Chippawa, Porter's force at the battle was a brigade in name only. By his own calculation, he brought no more than 300 men into action at Lundy's Lane. See Porter to Tompkins, July 29, 1814 in Cruikshank, *Documentary History*, I, p. 101.

"We never would surrender..."

ably elevated, which exposed them to the elevation that a musket ball will take in going any considerable distance, while their balls were passing high in the air over our heads. At length the call from the officers to cease firing and march forward was obeyed.

I had twenty rounds of cartridge in my box when I went to the battle ground, and when the firing ceased on examining my box I found that the last was in my musket. Cartridges and flints were now hastily distributed along the line, and our brave brigade, blackened with powder, marched forward toward the top of the hill to drive the enemy from his position there. In our march we passed over the dead and dying, who were literally in heaps, especially where the British had stood during the battle.

When we arrived at the top of the hill we came to a thicket where an old fence had been. Crossing this disordered the line considerably, and when through it we found ourselves within a few yards of the British, who were strongly reinforced and returning against us.

A death-like silence for a few moments prevailed, and both armies stood still. One of the British officers asked in a hoarse voice if we had surrendered. There was no answer to this question. He asked again. Lieutenant Dick told him that we *never would* surrender. The Canadian company on the right began to falter,[145] and, firing irregularly, the whole body fled back over the fence, the British complimenting us with a shower of musket balls. A number were killed and others were wounded in this tumultuous retreat. Running about fifteen or twenty rods we thought ourselves out of danger and several of us at the request of the officers stopped and were formed into line.

Col[onel]. Nicholas[146] had joined us that evening with a regiment of regulars, who had been kept in reserve, but now by skilful manoeuvres placed themselves between us and the British and kept up a destructive fire upon them until they fell back, and the firing ceased. A murmur which ran through the ranks of the volunteer companies, who were contending for places in the rear, and the groans of the dying was all that was heard for some minutes.

The shattered remains of the brigade being formed, we were marched to the right of the line and near the edge of the precipice of the Niagara Falls.[147] The cannon that had been taken from the British was at this place. We were formed in order of battle.

---

[145] A reference to Willcocks' Canadian Volunteers who were part of Porter's Brigade. If captured, they faced the hangman, a fact that made them somewhat shy of close-quarter combat.

[146] Lieutenant Colonel Roger C. Nicholas, 1st Infantry.

[147] This is an error. The location of the battle was quite distant from the Niagara River.

This to me was one of the most trying moments of my life. Being warm during the engagement I had opened my vest and shirt collar, and now the night air chilled me. Death, the common lot of all mankind, is generally feared the nearer it approaches us. I felt my situation to be an awful one, and I did sincerely wish that the British army, who were on the hill in view of us, might not come down to commence the engagement again. The British army retiring, our company with others were ordered to haul the cannon taken from the British and tumble it over the precipice. We hauled one and sent it over the precipice into the river.[148]

We then went back and were ordered to haul another, but being tired out and half dead for want of water, the most of our faces scorched with powder, we refused to do any more, and our officers led us back to our place in line.

A retrograde march back to the camp now commenced, the volunteers in front and the regulars in the rear to cover the retreat. When we arrived at the camp a number of men who had run off from us during the engagement came back and wished to fall into ranks, but were ordered off by Lieutenant Patton,[149] who had now command of the company.

The next thing [he did] was to make a speech to us. He began by saying he was surprised at us for not standing our ground at the bush fence. If the whole brigade had fled, (as they actually did) Gordon's company should have stood firm.

This was too much. We believed that we had done all that men could do, and this was our thanks. We broke loose on him with a volley of insulting language. He, standing in front of us, with a smile told us [we] were dismissed, and might go to the river and get drunk on the water.

I now learned that ten of our company were wounded. There was a number killed in every company but ours.[150] Thomas Poe, the Adjutant of the regiment, was mortally wounded. He was my full cousin, a man of fine talents, a brave and meritorious officer, and treated us like a brother.

---

[148] Actually this piece of artillery, a brass 6-pounder gun, was recovered by the United States Artillery and taken back to the camp at Chippawa. Today, it survives as a trophy piece at Fort McNair, near Washington, D.C.

[149] Second Lieutenant William Patton from Greencastle, Franklin County, Pennsylvania.

[150] The official casualty return for Fenton's Regiment on July 25, 1814 was 11 killed, 14 wounded and one missing. The official return for the Left Division showed 171 killed, 572 wounded and 117 missing. See Cruikshank, *Documentary History*, II, pp. 420-21.

6. The Retreat to Fort Erie

The next morning a scene of distress presented itself to my view, which I hope I may never witness again. I started early to see Thomas Poe, hearing he was lying in a house at Chippawa, a short distance from our camp. Calling at some of the tents as I passed along, I found that nearly all of them contained one or more wounded men, their clothes covered with blood and they were suffering severely. John McClay,[151] the Quartermaster, was wounded by a musket ball which cut him across the forepart of the head and cracked his skull. He was lying on his back, his face in a gore of blood. The strange, wild look and the deep groan he gave just as I entered drew a smile from me; so accustomed do men become to blood that they feel but little sympathy for their fellows.

Coming to the house at Chippawa, I found Thomas Poe lying on a blanket. He reached his hand to me and told me that he was mortally wounded, that he had but a few moments to live, and told me that he wished to be buried on the American side of the river.

The army at this time was on its march and passed the house, going to attack the British.[152] I had no wish to go with them as I had become satisfied the previous day, and, the officers telling me to stay and attend Poe, I stood in the door and with sorrow watched the shattered remains of only twenty-five out of the hundred that had left Franklin County as with slow and melancholy steps they were returning to the scene of the action.

In a short time the whole body returned, as it was found that the British were strongly reinforced and were preparing to attack us. Our troops had suffered severely the night before; especially one regiment that the evening before had paraded four hundred men now had but eighty-eight. Added to this, Major-General Brown, the commander, and Brigadier-General Scott, who commanded the first brigade, were both wounded, and the provisions were also destroyed. Lieutenant Campbell,[153] a number of regulars and myself carried the wounded Thomas Poe to the crossing place. Carrying him nearly a mile

---

[151] Captain John McClay or Maclay, regimental quartermaster of Fenton's Pennsylvanians.

[152] On the morning of July 26, 1814, Brigadier General Ripley, who had succeeded to command of the Left Division, marched on Brown's orders to the battlefield to recover the British artillery that had been abandoned (but for one piece) by the Americans the previous night. He advanced as far north as the Bridgewater Mills, two miles from the Chippawa, when he encountered the British drawn up in line of battle. Declining to engage, Ripley withdrew to Chippawa and, that afternoon, the Left Division retreated to Fort Erie. Brown never forgave his subordinate for his failure to repossess the British guns. See Graves, *The Battle of Lundy's Lane,* chapter 11.

[153] Possibly Second Lieutenant Henry M. Campbell, U.S. Corps of Artillery.

"I was now attacked with a high fever..."

across a plain, in the middle of the 26th of July, appeared to exhaust what little strength he had left. I put him in a boat in care of Lieutenant Dick[154] and his waiter.[155] He shook hands with me for the last time. He said to me in a weak voice: "Alexander, you will never see me again in this world." He expired in a few minutes.[156]

Loading the remaining part of the wounded now commenced, and there were at least forty two-horse wagons loaded with these unfortunate men. Their sufferings in this mode of conveyance seemed to be dreadful and their groans were distressing. I was now attacked with a high fever and violent headache, and had to give up my musket and knapsack and take a seat in a wagon, but the jolting almost deranged me. I then attempted to walk, but finding my strength failing and being behind our regiment, I lay down in front of a house in despair, not caring what became of me. The regulars passing at this time, one of their officers assisted me to rise and made one of his soldiers support me for a short distance. I then felt better, and was able to walk without support.

It was now dark. We came to a watch-house opposite the village of Black Rock, and I went into it. The night was cloudy and had the appearance of a storm. There were a number of stragglers here from different companies, and we all lay down on the floor and I soon fell asleep, but an officer of the regulars with some men soon ordered us out. He sent some of his men to conduct me to the meadow where my company was. He gave me a blanket, and I was compelled to lie down in a high fever just as the rain began to come down in torrents. This of all nights I had ever spent was the most dreadful.

In the morning I found myself lying in water two inches deep. I was so weak I could scarcely walk. I now went with the company to Fort Erie. This was a small fort of sods, in which there were many men at work digging and carrying sods to raise the fort higher and repair the bastions. My messmates insisted on me going across the river until I got better. An application was made to General Porter, and I crossed into the United States, after having been in Canada nearly two months.

I went to the hospital, and Lieutenant Dick, Peter Keefer, William Edwards, and myself got a tent by ourselves. Some time passed, when the

---

[154] First Lieutenant William Dick from Mercersburg, Franklin County, Pennsylvania.

[155] Poe's soldier servant.

[156] Poe was apparently granted his wish to be buried on United States soil. A monument to him was erected some time later in the garrison cemetery at Fort Niagara. In July 1814, however, that post was held by the British.

British crossed the river and attacked a small body of Kentucky riflemen.[157]

The main body being at Fort Erie, we left Buffalo and went about two miles to an Indian town belonging to the Seneca Indians, who had removed to another about two miles from this, which also belonged to them. The situation of the first mentioned village was pleasant, the houses of one-story and about sixteen feet square, with a porch in front the whole length of the house. A beautiful meadow, orchards and small fields of wheat surrounded the village. There appeared to be about twelve acres cleared land. The Indians had left this village a short time before in consequence of some their people catching the smallpox. They supposed that it belonged to the village, and left it, with all their furniture and rush mats, which was their bedding.

Staying here one night and part of a day, we learned that the danger was over. The British, 1,100 strong,[158] attempted to cross a small creek. The riflemen had thrown up a breastwork of logs within point blank shot of the ford, and being excellent marksmen and veterans, the British found it no easy matter to cross the creek, and after several ineffectual attempts re-embarked, having lost many killed and wounded. The rifle regiment lost but few, being protected by their breastworks.[159]

My companions now left me. The physician said my disease was the dumb ague.[160] I had a high fever during the night, but during the day was able to walk about, though very weak. The hospital was intended for the sick and wounded of Porter's brigade. The superintendent and his assistants were from the Pennsylvania Regiment. I suppose there might have been sixty of us here generally, though I never saw a list.

After leaving the hospital I took quarters in the jail in Buffalo, which was at that time used as a storehouse. The noise of repairing old muskets, firing, &c., at this place almost distracted me with headache. Lieutenant Dick procured board for me at the house of a respectable widow named St. John,

---

[157] This is an error. The riflemen were from Major Ludowick Morgan's battalion of the 1st U.S. Rifle Regiment.

[158] The British force, under the command of Colonel John G.P. Tucker of the 41st Regiment of Foot, actually consisted of only 600 men. See Harvey to Conran, August 2, 1814, National Archives of Canada, Record Group 8 I, vol. 685, 31.

[159] This is a fairly accurate summation of the engagement at Conjocta Creek on August 3, 1814. For an account of this action and its important effect on the 1814 campaign, see Graves, *The Battle of Lundy's Lane*, chapter 13.

[160] Ague was an intermittent, malarial-type fever. Illness of this sort, almost certainly caused by poor sanitation and fatigue, was common throughout the Niagara campaign. See Whitehorne, *While Washington Burned*, pp. 49-50.

three miles from Buffalo. Her husband had died some years before, and left her five children to support. They had some property in Buffalo, where they had kept tavern, but during the preceding winter the British had destroyed it all except one small frame house which they left her.[161] I received all the kindness I could ask. Our life was economical in the highest degree, and I believe was a great means of restoring my health. In a few days I visited Buffalo and saw such of our company as were in the hospital. I had the company of Major Wood and Adjutant Kean,[162] a New Yorker, and I soon began to feel at home.[163]

---

[161] Jarvis Hanks also noted the house of a Buffalo "widow woman" that had been spared by the British in December 1813.

[162] This officer cannot be identified from the information provided.

[163] McMullen's narrative ends here, and it is not known whether the original text contained a description of his return to Pennsylvania. There was probably not much more to the account as his company was mustered out of service at Buffalo on August 26, 1814.

About the Editor
Donald E. Graves

A Life Member of the Old Fort Niagara Association since 1979, Donald E. Graves is employed by the Directorate of History, Department of National Defence of Canada. A historian who specializes in the War of 1812, he is the author of two new tactical studies, *The Battle of Lundy's Lane: On the Niagara in 1814* and *Red Coats and Grey Jackets: The Battle of Chippawa, 5 July 1814*. He is also the editor of *Merry Hearts Make Light Days: The War of 1812 Memoir of Lieutenant John Le Couteur, 104th Foot*. His most recent publication is *Normandy 1944: The Canadian Summer*.

Donald Graves lives in Almonte, near Ottawa, Ontario, and, when not occupied with research and writing, pursues his two favorite hobbies of emu watching and viticulture.

Preserving History At Old Fort Niagara

Since 1927 the preservation and interpretation of Old Fort Niagara have been the goals of the Old Fort Niagara Association, Inc. The Association is a private, not-for-profit organization. Membership is open to anyone with an interest in the Fort and its long history. The Association operates Old Fort Niagara, a State Historic Site, in cooperation with the New York State Office of Parks, Recreation and Historic Preservation.

Old Fort Niagara Publications

Publications are an extension of the Old Fort Niagara Association's educational purpose. Created in 1984, the Publications Committee has been charged with establishing and maintaining an ongoing program of works relevant to the history of Old Fort Niagara. This includes new titles as well as the republication of older works.

Old Fort Niagara Association Publications Committee
Harry M. DeBan: Chairman/Publisher   Brian Leigh Dunnigan: Editor
Editorial Board:
David J. Bertuca; Craig O. Burt III; John Burtniak; Richard Cary, Jr.; Mark Francis; Patricia Rice

Additional information about the Fort's publications, exhibits, programs, or membership in the Old Fort Niagara Association may be obtained from:

Old Fort Niagara
Fort Niagara State Park
P.O. Box 169
Youngstown, New York 14174-0169

Soldiers of 1814: American Enlisted Men's Memoirs of the Niagara Campaign . . .
Production Coordinator: Harry M. DeBan
Production Editor: Brian Leigh Dunnigan
Production Support: David J. Bertuca, Craig O. Burt III, John Burtniak, Richard Cary, Jr., Mark Francis and Patricia Rice.
This book was printed in the United States of America on acid-free paper by:
Princeton Academic Press, Lawrenceville, New Jersey.